BOWMANVILLE

A SMALL TOWN AT THE EDGE

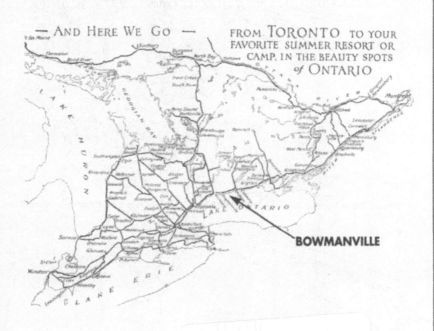

— And Here We Go —

FROM TORONTO TO YOUR FAVORITE SUMMER RESORT OR CAMP, IN THE BEAUTY SPOTS of ONTARIO

BOWMANVILLE

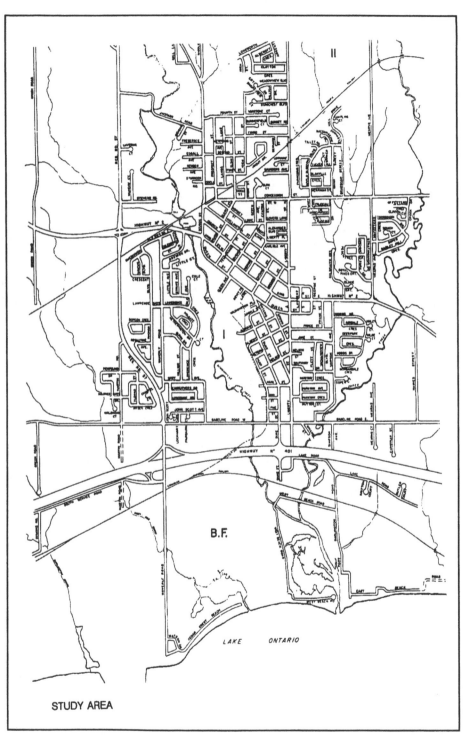

STUDY AREA

B.F.

LAKE ONTARIO

Bowmanville circa 1991.

BOWMANVILLE

A SMALL TOWN AT THE EDGE

William Humber

Natural Heritage Books

Bowmanville
A Small Town at the Edge
Published by Natural Heritage / Natural History Inc.
P.O. Box 95, Station O,
Toronto, Ontario M4A 2M8

Design by Steve Eby

Canadian Cataloguing in Publication Data
Humber, William, 1949—
    Bowmanville: a small town at the edge

Includes bibliographical references and index.
ISBN 1-896219-21-7

1. Bowmanville (Clarington, Ont.) - History. I. Title.

FC3099.B685H85 1997   971.3'56 C97-930511-X
F1059.5.B685H85 1997

THE CANADA COUNCIL | LE CONSEIL DES ARTS
FOR THE ARTS | DU CANADA
SINCE 1957 | DEPUIS 1957

Natural Heritage / Natural History Inc. acknowledges the support received for
its publishing program from the Canada Council Block Grant Program. We
also acknowledge with gratitude the assistance of the Association for the
Export of Canadian Books, Ottawa, and the office of the Ontario Arts
Council, Toronto.

Table of Contents

Acknowledgments vii

The Brick Town: An Introduction ix

One: The Land is a Narrative 1

Two: The Deed of Conveyance 4

Three: The Building Blocks of Settlement 8

Four: Few More Picturesque Spots In Ontario 13

Five: Our Bank 19

Six: Genuine Original Men are Scarce 23

Seven: Places of Grace 41

Eight: Not Afraid to Face Public Opinion 55

Nine: A Drowsy State of Existence 64

Ten: The Lives of Ordinary People 71

Eleven: He Has Done Some Good in the Community 78

Twelve: Town Landmark Gives Way
    to Community Progress 89

Thirteen: The Town Which Nobody Leaves 98

Fourteen: If It Sticks to Its Principles 103

Photo Credits 121

Appendix A 124

Appendix B 125

Index 127

Scenes from present day Bowmanville

Acknowledgments

Writing a small town's story presents problems that other types of histories avoid, particularly if one is a resident of that town. One risks offending some while angering others for neglecting their place in the town's past. Having said that however the opportunity to express both affection for common places and experiences, and occasional criticism of inappropriate decision-making, is one that one would not wish to avoid.

I begin by noting my debt to the many fine histories of the town written over the years including Coleman's *History of the Early Settlement of Bowmanville and Vicinity*, Fairbairn's *History and Reminiscences of Bowmanville*, Squair's *The Townships of Darlington and Clarke*, Hamlyn, Lunney and Morrison's *Bowmanville: A Retrospect*, the various editors of Picture the Way We Were, and Leetooze's *The First 200 Years: A Brief History of Darlington Township*.

My greatest debt however was to the inestimable *Canadian Statesman* newspaper, whose pages over the years brim with the life of the community. I say it elsewhere in this book and repeat it here, that in many ways Bowmanville is the "Canadian Statesman" and it would be hard to imagine one without the other.

Among the folks who have given advise, ideas and inspiration I mention only a few when so many are entitled to recognition. Garfield Shaw has collected as fine a pictorial record of a small town as exists anywhere. Garth Gilpin of the Bowmanville Business Area and Charles Taws of the Bowmanville Museum have read this manuscript in its early stages and provided helpful commentary. Neighbours and friends Marjorie and Eileen Couch and Muriel Crago have helped in many unseen but significant ways.

Institutional support from among others, Central Public School, including my former co-author Doris Falls, the Bowmanville Museum, and Bowmanville Branch of the Clarington Public Library have been invaluable.

My wife Cathie and children Bradley, Darryl and Karen share in the experience of living in Bowmanville. I salute another distant relative and wonderful popular historian, and the man I refer to as Mr. Bowmanville, Stu Candler to whose memory this book is dedicated.

I acknowledge, the many important writers including Garrison Keillor, William Least-Heat Moon, Peter Ackroyd, James Kunstler, Simon Schama and others whose words have influenced my own interpretation of the history and life of a small town and a special place.

I remember, in conclusion, my mother who gave me the love for reading and writing. Her inspiration will always be part of me.

A classic photo of Bowmanville's Market Square, celebrating Queen Victoria's Diamond Jubilee, 24 May 1897.

The Brick Town

An Introduction

"In Bowmanville we had quite a gala day on Thursday last,
when the Fireman's Annual Gathering took place. The "brick
town" has seldom looked so gay or lively."
—The Gossiper, The Canadian Statesman, 12 September 1872

"To palliate the shortness of our lives, and to compensate our
brief time in this world, it is fit to have such an understanding
of times past that we may be considered to have dwelled in the
same. In such manner, answering the present with the past, we
may live from the beginning and in a certain sense be as old as
our country itself.
—Peter Ackroyd, English Music

"A rationale extension of bygone religious systems, fairy tales,
and above all of psychoanalysis into architectural expression
becomes more urgent every day."
—Ivan Chtcheglov, as quoted in "Lipstick Traces" (Greil Marcus)

Long time residents, particularly those born in Bowmanville, often seem to
pronounce their hometown's name as "Boneville". The Canadian Statesman
once reported that a New England newspaper used that spelling because a
reporter interpreted it this way after interviewing an old lady who had been
born here.

A local history can not avoid being at least partially an exercise in this kind
of nostalgia—a looking back to a supposed golden age in which folks met each
other daily on the town's streets, were proud of their home town and shared
common institutions like their local public school where they met those both
like themselves and different. Nevermind that the reality was often at odds
with the memory. It at least had to have elements of truth to be preserved in
such sepia tones.

The story of Bowmanville, Ontario contained in these pages is told from a
point of view. The past may not have been as rose-hued as we'd like to imagine, but it had real elements of public affinity in which folks saw themselves as
part of a larger polity, one based on human comradeship and not the private
pursuit of consumer identity.

One can read different points of view today which suggest either that we are
returning to a more clamorous public sense of obligation and lifestyle, or another which argues that our real destiny is a soothing, mall-like existence of private
realities.

What is particularly apparent, however, is that regardless of what takes place (and it will probably be a mixture of the polar opposites), successful urban living, as opposed to that which just gets by as a collection of gated communities and monster stores, will be based on the uniqueness and community spirit of a place. It will embody what James Kunstler calls, "chronological connectivity"—in which the past is allied with a vision for the future. The development of these types of places, now commonly referred to as renaissance communities, is controlled to a greater extent than might be thought by local residents.

This book is intended to be an archive of memory restoring a picture of Bowmanville's past and suggesting means through which a local renaissance could be formulated. As such it is often critical and harsh in its judgement, but at the same time generous in its appreciation of the errors and intentions of past actions.

We cannot escape our past, but its joys and sorrows are such that we should not want to do so. Maybe it is pure fantasy to imagine that local streetcorners could be invested with tales of whimsy, but if it can be for Italian landscapes or a Brooklyn neighbourhood, where myth informs almost every turn in the road and which are distinguished by local idioms and foods, than why not so for a Canadian place.

Bowmanville is at the edge of the Toronto region and as such its identity as a small town may not exist for long in the future. It may be positioned to become simply one additional residential enclave for a larger region—one which has no special character. Or it may, if it so chooses, select a future based on building a unique image from the town's own history. In so doing it could become the kind of place people travel for miles to visit, businesses crave the opportunity to locate in and where common people celebrate their style of living. We've all visited these kinds of places, usually on holidays. My particular favourite is Cooperstown, New York which would be just as wonderful even if the Baseball Hall of Fame was not there.

The fact that film makers continue to use Bowmanville for their productions which in recent years have included *The Private Capital* and *Wind at My Back*, suggest that some have noticed the town's special quality.

Change is a constant. Just as the area's native population gradually departed, so has the sentimental old town of Bowmanville lost its antique character. In the process, however, its very name is now threatened and a burgeoning and perhaps inevitable population growth often seems to have little connection to past tradition.

This book asks, perhaps idealistically, why can we not design the future life and appearance of Bowmanville to conform to its authentic past? Why not plant classic trees on new streets to match the wonderful old oak tree that survives on Beech Avenue? Why not configure new streets to match the present grid system that links neighbourhoods of varying backgrounds? In combination with major streets crossing the grid at an angle why not create odd parcels of land such as are found in the old part of town? Why not mix land uses so that a resident of a new subdivision could walk to a corner store or community centre? Why not lobby to have trains run locals to downtown Toronto as they once did? These are pictures from the imagination. There are dozens of these examples from Bowmanville's history in which the past can live in the present.

I admit of a certain affection for Bowmanville and environs based both on a family history with the area and a more recent residence. I have been told by one historian that the first Humbers in North America were based in Bowmanville, but had left by the early 20th century. More significantly my mother's family on her father's side descended from the Candlers, the family of one of Bowmanville's esteemed 20th century citizens, Stuart Candler.

As a citizen of Bowmanville since 1974 and a resident of Beech Avenue, which I have no hesitation in describing as one of the wonderful little streets of the world, I have watched a brief period of the town's history in which some of its unique businesses such as the Glen Rae Dairy have disappeared while other companies such as the local foundry were saluted in 1996 as examples of industrial excellence.

Changes in the Province of Ontario's planning laws in 1996 threaten the fumbling attempts to re-write the design of urban places in which a denser urban fabric, community connection and inter-related land uses might have been found. It is clear, however, that the realization of such a vision will never be initially determined by legislated convention, but will emerge only from public sentiment.

This book is intended to be an affectionate ramble through Bowmanville's past as an instructive preview of a community life based on the fullest and most authentic demonstration of human living.

Bowmanville began life in the late 18th century in the valley of the Bowmanville Creek below the present day Vanstone Mill and was known, among other names, as Darlington Mills. It spread east along the present Highway two and through the 1830s, gradually becoming known as Bowmanville. With independent municipal status as a town obtained in 1858, it was located in the south end of Darlington Township which in turn was part of the western edge of Durham County, itself a part of the combined counties of Northumberland and Durham.

Significantly in 1852 two brothers, Alsay and Thomas Fox, produced brick from land roughly conforming to the present Memorial Park. With new houses and businesses being built daily, the demand was brisk such that by 1872 the anonymous Gossiper writing in *The Statesman* referred to Bowmanville as "The Brick Town." While others used the description of "the cow town" in reference to the running at large of cows in the south ward, I prefer the more prosaic and tactile image of the brick town as a metaphor for Bowmanville, even though some locals noted the brick was not always of the best quality and has tended to crumble on application of cleansing compounds.

Bowmanville remained in its 19th century political form until 1974 when it was combined with the townships of Darlington and Clarke to become the Town of Newcastle, one of eight area municipalities in the Region of Durham. The Town of Newcastle's name was changed to the Municipality of Clarington in 1993 and Bowmanville remains a part of that jurisdiction.

Chapter One

The Land is a Narrative

"...landscape is the work of the mind. Its scenery is built up as much from strata of memory as from layers of rock."
– Simon Schama, *Landscape and Memory*

"The land is a narrative"
– William Least-Heat Moon, *Prairyerth*

"We understand the width of the world, but its age is beyond our grasp "
– Phil Jenkins, *An Acre of Time*

May is the most tranquil and loveliest of months in Ontario as new life and soft greens crowd the landscape. In 1842 settlement and the destruction of the original forest left a scarred and often dispirited scene. The old wilderness was in sad retreat, but it had yet to be replaced wholly by the patchwork quilt pattern of fields, small woodlots, hedgerows, wooden fences and brick homes which would characterize our image and fond memory of southern Ontario.

In that spring Charles Dickens and his wife Catherine from whom he would one day cruelly separate, took a break from the novelist's exhausting literary tour of America to visit Toronto and then travel on to Montreal. Of the Ontario countryside Dickens would later write, "There was the swamp, the bush, the perpetual chorus of frogs, the rank unseemly growth, the unwholesome steaming earth."[1] The idea was informed by the total experience of Ontario and we will never know if on that trip to Montreal he slept on the portion of the journey past Bowmanville or was able to view it with any degree of fascination.

The desultory appearance of the fledgling British colony marked the final stages of the destruction of what had been there only fifty years previously. John Squair described its features as consisting of "...the rich and varied forest growth...on the best clay loam soils it was essentially a beech and maple forest...on the lighter, sandy soils also there was often a fine growth of hardwood...in the wet lands, such as in the bottoms of valleys eroded by the streams, there were splendid areas of white cedar, with a large percentage of birch, elm, ash, basswood, pine and hemlock, and, sometimes, in the wettest places, the tamarack."[2]

This was the world that had been populated by aboriginal inhabitants and was virtually undisturbed except for necessary pathways such as that from the

1

site of present day Bowmanville north to Lake Scugog. This Indian trail passing through the future locations of Hampton and Enniskillen would one day become what is now known as the "Old Scugog Road."

But there was a time before even the immense darkness of the forest and its native population, when the region was covered by the last Ice Age. A glacial sheet covered all of this territory so that it resembled the gravest portions of the Arctic and Antarctic. According to *The Canadian Encyclopedia* this Ice Age conformed to the Pleistocene epoch of geologic time, "…during which periodic, extensive glacial activity occurred in many parts of the world. This period began two to three million years ago and lasted until 10,000 years before the present."[3] It is the conceit of humankind that the life of several million years can be reduced to so little space in the history of an area.

As the Ice Age slowly closed the glacial sheet stopped at a point which, in the area of Bowmanville, conformed to what would be the northern concessions of Darlington and Clarke Townships. A great ridge of deposits was left here to become the Pine Ridge and below which the springs arose which flow south as the two main creeks, Bowmanville and Soper, which define Bowmanville's old western and eastern boundaries.

The ice continued its retreat, and as it did and temperatures rose, a great lake known as Iroquois filled a basin to the south which conforms to present Lake Ontario. It was in fact larger and covered the southern parts of the later township of Darlington to a point roughly equivalent to the fourth concession. All of Bowmanville as we know it was underwater.

Boys skating on the frozen pond of the Vanstone Mill, December 26, 1916. This picture provides an excellent view of the west end of town at the time.

As the lake fell to its present level the land's lacustrine sand and clay were exposed. The sand and gravel which lay to the north were cut by creeks flowing south, creating the valleys and hills which characterize the area.[4] The inter-lobate moraine left by the ice age proved to be an excellent aquifer for well water north of Bowmanville.

Underlying all of this, and the oldest feature of the entire area, are the Ordovician rocks of the Cobourg, Collingwood and Gloucester formations. According to the 1962 study by School of Architecture students at the University of Toronto, "Well records indicate that the depth to bedrock varies from a minimum of 54 feet to a maximum of 200 feet or more."[5]

This rock, part of the very foundation of planet earth, will remain long after any trace of the present community has been washed away by time.

Notes

[1] Edwin Guillet, *The Story of Canadian Roads.* (Toronto: University of Toronto Press, 1966), p. 52.

[2] John Squair, *The Townships of Darlington and Clarke.* (Toronto: University of Toronto Press, 1927), p.2.

[3] N.W. Rutter, "Ice Age," *The Canadian Encyclopedia* Second Edition. (Edmonton: Hurtig Publishers, 1988).

[4] Squair, p. 1.

[5] Students of the Division of Town and Regional Planning, School of Architecture, University of Toronto, *Official Plan for the Town of Bowmanville* (1962), p. 11.

Chapter Two

A Deed of Conveyance

*"I believe Indians fear loss of meaning—that is, memory—
beyond all other losses, because without it one can love
nothing. After all love proceeds from memory, and
survival depends absolutely upon memory."*
– William Least-Heat Moon, *Prairyerth*

Change is never some anonymous, inevitable force acting like a law of
nature. It is at least partially, and often largely, the result of human actions
and choice. Such was the fate of the original native inhabitants.

There appear to have been few natives in the area at any time. Residence
may have been limited to the summer when creeks flowing into Lake Ontario
were stocked with fish.[1] That use corresponds to the recreation of later
Bowmanville citizens for whom fishing in the Bowmanville Creek below the
Vanstone Mill is perhaps their strongest authentic connection with the surrounding environment.

According to archaeological evidence native contact with the area dates to the
European time of 1000 BC, often referred to as the Woodland Period. From perhaps 700 BC to 1000 AD the Point Peninsula Culture covered this area and much
of Eastern Ontario. Ontario Iroquois then dominated much of southern Ontario
from 1000 AD to the coming of European contact. Their lifestyle was characterized by a corn economy supplemented by fishing and hunting. By 1400 the combination of beans and squash with corn diminished their reliance on hunting.

Contact between Europeans and natives began in Ontario in the 17th century, but such encounters would have been casual and rare in the area of
Bowmanville in this period. Still, arrowheads and pottery fragments occasionally rise up from the earth to remind present day residents of a native presence.
In her remarks on returning to Bowmanville for centennial celebrations in
1958, Minnie Jennings recalled an old Indian burial ground at the site of the
Medland home on Liberty Street. She also told stories that had been the mate-
rial of her own youth about a native battleground on the Vanstone's Hill, with
a tribe on the hill attacking a tribe as it came down what would become the
Kingston Road. "My brother and I found several Indian arrow heads as we
played in Mr. Horsey's Grove or gathered beech nuts under the trees," she said.[2]

These events, however, occurred before formal white settlement and in fact
disease and war had practically ended the Iroquois presence by 1650. There
would be about one hundred years of virtual non-population marking the

boundary between one residency and the next in this area. Formal native contact in the area around Bowmanville with Europeans and American ex-patriates began in the late 18th century, and the earliest reports of contact generally suggest an amicable if uneasy co-habitation.

James Fairbairn says that scattered bands of Rice Lake natives hunted along the creeks "...but never interfered with the white people appearing quite harmless and kindly disposed."[3] John Coleman on the other hand shows his sympathies early in his little history of Bowmanville, referring to "...the rude, savage Indian, who looked with jealous eyes upon the encroachment of the whites."[4] He proceeds to build a case for the original white settlers' bravery against enormous odds noting, "The Indians were very troublesome, and caused considerable anxiety, being armed and equipped, and very different from the remnants of the broken tribes occasionally seen at the present time."[5] To support his case, however, he lamely describes one instance in which the home of one of the three original settling families, the Trulls, was invaded by a native woman and her four children. Only Mrs. Trull and her children were home and the native woman asked for some flour which was denied. She proceeded to search the house and distribute the flour in equal portions to the white family and hers.[6] It may have been a type of communalism unacceptable to the new inhabitants but it also suggests a necessary justice in a time of want.

Most accounts of native-white contact in the 19th century focus on a dispirited even tragic remnant of a people and treat them as objects of bizarre humour and racial contempt. One such account from *The Observer* in 1878 described a lacrosse game at the Drill Shed on present day Carlisle Avenue in which, "An Indian, Johnnie Cornstalk, with his squaw came to the game drunk and when heckled he threw a brick that cracked the skull of his spouse. She was attended by Dr. McLaughlin and was taken home to the wigwam where she is recovering."[7]

Nevertheless the British tried to acknowledge the basic native ownership of these lands even though such European concepts were of limited or non-existent import among aboriginals in North America for whom land was a sacred trust not a commodity to be bought and sold. Occupancy was not a factor of market forces but usually resulted from superior military resolve.

In 1775, following the acquisition of France's lands in the New World, but also cognizant of future problems with the thirteen colonies in America and the need to retain native alliances, the British superiors of Governor Carleton instructed that:

"No purchase of Lands belonging to the Indians, whether in the Name and for the use of the Crown, or in the Name and for the Use of proprietaries of Colonies be made but at some general Meeting, at which the principal chiefs of each tribe, claiming a property in such Lands, are present; and all Tracts, so purchased, shall be regularly surveyed by a Sworn Surveyor in the presence and with the Assistance of a person deputed by the Indians to attend such Survey;

Vanstone's Pond, Bowmanville, Ontario.

and the said Surveyor shall make an accurate Map of such Tract, describing the Limits, which Map shall be entered upon Record, with the Deed of Conveyance from the Indians."[8]

These explicit directions were ignored almost immediately in a large territory which included the present site of Bowmanville. In 1783, following the victory by American insurgents and the British need to relocate thousands of Loyalists on the very native land which they hoped to acquire, Sir John Johnson was appointed to oversee Indian affairs.

On October 9 of that year, following a meeting of several Mississauga leaders and British military administrators on Carleton Island at the east end of Lake Ontario, Captain Crawford reported to Johnson that, "He had purchased from the Mississaugas all the land from Toniato or Onagara to the River in the Bay of Quinte within eight leagues of the bottom of the said Bay, including all of the islands, extending from the lake back as far as a man can travel in a day."[9]

But there remained something untoward about the negotiations. Even as details faded it was clear that despite Carleton's instructions, Crawford had used questionable means to convince the natives to sign what was effectively a blank deed for the area from the Etobicoke Creek west of Toronto to the Trent River, to a depth of ten to twelve miles from Lake Ontario. Popularly dubbed the "Gun Shot Treaty" it had no follow-up survey or legal description. Sir John Johnson hushed up the indiscretion by forbidding any staff associated with the Indian Department to benefit from the transaction.

Though lands in the Toronto area between the Don and Etobicoke Creek were part of the Toronto Purchase Treaty in 1787 and later confirmed in 1805, the majority of Gun Shot Treaty lands including those on which Bowmanville sits, remained part of the controversial earlier deal.

An 1847 map of Indian surrendered land reaffirmed the native position that they had never signed away the area, but the government was faced with significant white settlement in the area which made retrenchment unlikely. They maintained that the natives had effectively acquiesced to the state of affairs. The issue might have forever remained in legal ambiguity but for embarrassing questions arising out of native land claims in British Columbia in the 1920s. Land issues were reopened in other parts of the country including those associated with the Gun Shot Treaty's invalidity, "a fact" historian Leo Johnson says, "of which even the Mississaugas were not aware."[10]

Indians of the day were affectively wards of the very Crown now called upon to resolve the land issue. The Williams Commission appointed in 1923 "negotiated" the purchase of disputed lands in Ontario including those of Bowmanville for a mere half million dollars and natives gave up all "right, title, interest, claim, demand or privileges" to the areas in dispute.[11] Obviously this represented only a fraction of the 1923 value of the land, but with the signing of various treaties native interest in the land on which Bowmanville sits was finally resolved.

Notes

[1] J.B. Fairbairn, *History and Reminiscences of Bowmanville*. (Bowmanville News Print, 1906), p. 3.

[2] *The Canadian Statesman*, 26 June 1958.

[3] J.B. Fairbairn, *History and Reminiscences of Bowmanville*. p. 3.

[4] J.T. Coleman, *History of the Early Settlement of Bowmanville and Vicinity*. (Bowmanville: 1875), p. 4.

[5] Ibid, p.5

[6] Ibid, p. 5–6

[7] From *The Observer*, 1878, as quoted in The Canadian Statesman, 4 February 1948.

[8] Leo Johnson, *History of the County of Ontario 1615-1875*. (Whitby: Corporation of the County of Ontario, 1973), p. 20–21.

[9] Ibid, p. 23

[10] Ibid, p. 31

[11] Ibid, p. 34

Chapter Three

The Building Blocks of Settlement

*"No mapping has ever so profoundly affected the physical
appearance of land as did the township surveying method."*
– William Least-Heat Moon, *Prairyerth*

The Four Corners of Bowmanville, at King and Temperance Streets, before 1900.
The grid layout of streets and alignment of King Street (Highway 2) shaped the
streetscape of Bowmanville. The Town Hall is over stores in centre of picture, with
Market Square, Fire Hall, and bandshell in background.

Ontario (1867-present) which has had so many identities as Canada West
(1841-67) and before that Upper Canada (1791-1841), was, in its first
European interpretation, a part of the province of Québec (1763-91).
Restrictions on freehold land ownership and a Gallic-based Civil Code of
justice marked this region as a quasi-colony of a largely French speaking territory following the cession of Québec to British Authority in 1763.

In 1788 Lord Dorchester proclaimed four German-titled districts, named
after branches of the Hanoverian dynasty, to administer the largely unpopu-
lated region of what is now Ontario. One of those four districts, Nassau, later
named the Home District, included the land on which the future town of
Bowmanville grew.[1] Three years later the future province would gain its independence with the creation of Upper and Lower Canada.

The naming process was a powerful tool of Empire. In 1792 counties were set
out bearing the names of English counterparts, but they had little real authority though they did contain within them the township system of survey within
which orderly settlement could occur.

Districts remained the primary form of local government through the first
half of the 19th century, but even they were realigned to conform with townships and ensure that no settler was more than a day's journey from the place

in which they discharged their public duties. For the purposes of Bowmanville's future the town's site resided in the Township of Darlington in the County of Durham (part of the future combined counties of Northumberland and Durham) which in turn was part of the District of Newcastle.

Settlers from the United States had been entering the new territory since the American Revolution and Major Samuel Holland, Surveyor General, administered the immediate laying out and posting of frontages, or baselines, of townships on rivers and lakes. This was followed by the blocking out on paper of lands stretching back into the wilderness. Their physical realization would have to wait.[2]

What was significant about this grid was less the character of individual roads than the net structure formed by all of the roads in combination. This landscape was far from the rural Ontario we are familiar with today. Roads were almost impassable and the key attribute of a horse was its ability to swim. Conditions were so inhospitable that Upper Canada was described as "a vile country of low people."[3]

The principle method of land subdivision reflected a desire to impose a pattern of order and rationality on an area of solitary wilderness within which the reaches of empire would be felt. Townships were laid out along Lake Ontario with the exception of those branching out from Yonge Street. Along the lake they were nine miles in width and twelve miles in depth. Such was the pattern in the range of townships surveyed in 1791 between the River Trent and the Toronto Purchase and confirmed in Simcoe's declaration of 26 July 1792. Lots were a 1/4 mile wide and concessions a mile and a quarter mile deep to give a desired two-hundred acre lot.

Parts of Darlington were surveyed in 1793 and 1797. It was a serious business in which the surveyor recorded the quality of soil, number of rock outcroppings and types of timber. Anyone who pulled down or defaced a survey monument was subject to "death without benefit of clergy."[4]

There was nothing arbitrary about the mile and a quarter separation. It came from English mathematician Edmund Gunter's original chain measuring device created in the early 17th century which in turn derived from the old Roman rod measurement of sixteen and half feet. A hundred links added up to one chain of sixty-six feet (four Roman rods) and one-hundred of these chains conformed to the concession separation. A mile was eighty chains. A highway grant was laid out as one chain with a roadbed of usually forty feet in the middle. The standard length of a section of rail fence was eleven feet, or one-sixth chain. A canal way was a chain in width, telegraph poles would later be one or two chains apart and a city block was three chains to a block and one to a street. In the layout of townships a sideline road was placed at forty chain distances allowing for the provision of two two-hundred acre lots within the boundaries of a concession road and sideline, an acre being ten square chains.

A later view of the Four Corners, showing buildings which with the exception of the Town Hall in the background have now been demolished.

Aerial view of Bowmanville.

Each township had a base line as the preliminary building block to allow the territory to escape the meandering natural boundary of the lake. It was a vision of empire in which the formality of the grid and town replaced the anarchy of wilderness. In the original visions a town would grow in the centre of each township along this baseline and further roads would be spaced at mile and quarter postings from the original baseline.

This was the perfect pattern upon which the region that included Bowmanville was supposed to grow. But the intention of a town on the baseline was impractical, perhaps because the baseline was not far enough from the lake, and because of its associated topographical peculiarities and swampy conditions. Asa Danforth's east-west road was closer to the second concession and along this second front the entrepreneurial imagination of first arrivals founded many of the major towns east of Toronto including Pickering, Whitby, Oshawa and Bowmanville.[5] A river, a mill and a fordable site for the road combined to create the conditions for Bowmanville's establishment.

The rise of important 19th century Ontario towns was furthered by the School Act in 1846 and then the Municipal Act in 1849 which replaced District government with that of counties. These acts led to a building boom of new courts, town halls and schools which were the necessary infrastructure, along with the first crude industrial buildings and stores, for the creation of town permanence.

Eventually money from wheat production in the rural hinterland brought builders, bricklayers and carpenters to small towns like Bowmanville and created the varied economy of rural Ontario. Wheat growing was in turn replaced by a more diversified farming economy as the century advanced. Ultimately small patchwork-like divisions of land into ten to twelve acres with hedgerows, treelines, and wooden snake fences created the distinctive appearance and pattern found in country areas.[6]

Most significantly in 1850, Northumberland and Durham Counties were united and assumed their legal place. Until 1974 Bowmanville's important political ties would be with eastern neighbours. This orientation influenced the future development of the town which left the valley of the Bowmanville Creek and began to follow the Kingston Road on its march to Port Hope and Cobourg.

Notes

1 George W. Spragge, "The Districts of Upper Canada 1788-1849," *Ontario History* XXXIX. (1947), pp. 91-100.

2 Don Thomson, *Men and Meridians: History of Surveying and Mapping in Canada.* (Ottawa: Queen's Printer, 1966).

3 Edwin Guillet, *The Story of Canadian Roads.* (Toronto: University of Toronto Press, 1966), p. 51.

4 W.F. Weaver, *Crown Surveys in Ontario.* (Ontario Department of Lands and Forests, 1962, revised 1968).

5 John van Nostrand, "Roads and Planning: The settlement of Ontario's Pickering Township, 1789-1975", *City Magazine,* 1975.

6 Blake and Greenhill, *Rural Ontario.* (Toronto: University of Toronto Press, 1969).

Chapter Four

Few More Picturesque Spots
in Ontario

*"...there are very few, if any, more picturesque spots in the
Province of Ontario. The principal part of the town is built
upon a high ridge of land running north and south overlooking
Lake Ontario and the lovely valley that intervenes. There
are two streams—one to the east and one to the west thus
affording good natural drainage."*
– J.B. Fairbairn, *History and Reminiscences of Bowmanville*

Lieutenant-Governor John Graves Simcoe first proclaimed the basis of survey, land ownership and purpose for Upper Canada on 7 February 1792. He desired the establishment of a landed aristocracy which would lead new settlement in the ways of loyalty to the institutions and ideals of Great Britain.

Squair says that while Simcoe's immediate intention was not realized "...freemen have lived upon that land and eaten abundantly of its fruits in peace, have inhabited good houses, have chosen their own councils and parliaments with full powers to make and unmake laws, and still have not run riot in tearing down the old barriers of authority in religion and morals. They have not demanded to be detached from Britain and her monarchy. Simcoe would not have asked for a higher result,...".[1]

The original settlers of the region about Bowmanville are celebrated rightly for their fortitude and imagination in choosing to relocate from the United States. But their long term role in the creation and evolution of the town are overrated dramatically in all local histories. Bowmanville's physical growth is of greater significance to present day residents than even the role of first settlers, for it shapes not only memory but the everyday experience of the town.

The first settlers were a second generation of United Empire Loyalists,[2] people as much concerned with acquiring virgin lands as with using them as collateral in their eventual assumption of a privileged position in what remained of British North America. They encountered hardship and strife, but in the main theirs was to be a life of advantage and opportunity in which the fortunes of the future community were of either limited or no import.

The Conants or Conats (the spelling depending on the source) and Trulls played only a minor role in Bowmanville's eventual story. However, the Burks or Burkes were somewhat more significant assuming on 31 December 1798, after completion of survey, Lot 13 Concession 1 as well as Lot 13 Broken Front, an area totalling four-hundred acres.[3] This contained within it the swift flowing creek on which a succession of mills most notably Vanstone's would be built. A tannery, carding mill, and other businesses would appear below this site on the west bank of the creek marking it as the area's first significantly settled and developed site.

The town, however, would not grow here despite the Belden Atlas' designation in 1878 of several streets, Coleman, Chapel and Clinton, below the millpond.[4] Today it is an uninhabited conservation area, but its westerly orientation is finally being realized in the strip highway development sprouting along Highway 2.

By 1820 John Burk had added a store to the grist mill and saw mill on his site. He sold the store about this time to a Lewis Lewis, a man of whom so little is known that it may be that his first or last name was used for both purposes.

In 1824 the business empire of Charles Bowman purchased the store. Bowman, a Scotsman based in Montreal, was an early dry goods entrepreneur and financier with interests throughout Ontario. Robert Fairbairn was sent to represent Bowman's interest and a year later a teenager, John Simpson (1812-1885), was hired as clerk. Simpson may in fact have been Bowman's illegitimate son. Bowmanville perhaps numbered about 118, but the personalities who would play key roles in its future were now in place.[5] Fairbairn left Bowman's employ to become Darlington's postmaster in 1829, the office having been re-located to Bowmanville two years before. Simpson, despite his age, now assumed a leading role in protecting Bowman's interests.

The small community which had begun life in the valley south of the present Vanstone Mill, was at first known simply as Darlington Mills. Here in the 1830s, according to Hamlyn, Lunney, and Morrison "...the settlement of Darlington and the adjoining townships got seriously underway, hundreds of immigrants coming in, mainly from the British Isles."[6] It was in this period that locals started to refer to the town by the name of the man whose store gave credit in times of need. Thomas Rolph's *Descriptive and Statistical Account of Canada* (1841) refers to "Bowmansville... as likely to be a large place."[7] Squair suggests the spelling was in error, but it seems more likely that by the 1830s people were calling Darlington Mills by the informal title of Bowman's village, and gradually over the next few years and with several interpretations, the more formal and present spelling was accepted as the preferred name.

Bowman himself had only limited contact with the village and eventually returned to England to pursue his interest in collecting European art. He died in the late 1840s, perhaps unaware of his legacy in the new world.

So homogeneous is the earliest European settlement of Bowmanville that Fairbairn devotes a paragraph to the first non-white, other than native, resident. "The first barber shop," he says, "was opened in a little hole dug out under

Turn of the century postcard scene of Bowmanville from the west.

the first hotel, occupied by Hindes. The professor of the tonsorial art was a colored man named Smith. He was tall, straight and muscular, something of a pugilist, and up to all kinds of circus performances. He was here, off and on till well up in the sixties. The only other colored family resident at this time was called Campbell." [8] Smith married one of the Campbell daughters and their son came back to Bowmanville many years later as an itinerant Methodist preacher.

In the area of Bowmanville, development at first seems to have been mainly on the western hill in the valley south of the present Vanstone Mill where, three or more stores, a large tavern and a cooper's shop were located. [9]

Of that first community, David Morrison Sr. wrote in 1939, "There were several houses down that way (in the valley) and today they are all gone except one lone brick dwelling which was then known as Williams' home...(the valley) was the principle business section of this corporation where besides an oatmeal mill there was also the Jacob Nead's Foundry..a woodworking shop, and a machine shop. All those works got their power from the dam below the bridge ... Then there was Gifford's Tannery...The Milne Distillery with its long rows of cattle sheds...The soap making works... The old pottery works on the west part to the Vanstone Pond. The big departmental Burk Store, and the Squair Grocery Store." [10]

The second piece of major importance for the future appearance of Bowmanville was the land transportation system. The first major east-west road in Upper Canada, as has been noted, was contracted to an American, Asa Danforth, in 1798 for a roadway forty feet wide between Kingston and Burlington. It cut across the future site of Bowmanville a short distance south of the present Highway 2. Absentee landlords on much of its progress throughout

Ontario soon ensured the road's general decline. Following the War of 1812 a new highway, the Kingston Road, was built from Kingston to present day Toronto following in many cases the old Danforth road.

In Bowmanville it crossed at an angle somewhat north of the older road, perhaps to take advantage of better crossing points on the east and west creeks. The layout of streets, parallel and in line with the Kingston Road and others in line with the north-south/east-west grid, parallel to Liberty and Concession streets, created Bowmanville's distinctive layout of irregular sized blocks of land and street directions.[11]

The third piece was the ownership of Lot 11. According to Squair, in 1828 the Crown granted the University of Toronto this four-hundred acre strip of land, a quarter mile wide, bound on the east by Liberty Street running from Lake Ontario to present day Concession Street.[12] This land conforms to Bowmanville's core and its sale to raise funds for the university made possible the town's eastward growth.

A similar scene of Bowmanville from the west. This time a very interesting shot of the town from afar, copied from what might have been a panoramic camera print. Presence of town hall in skyline, and other features, indicates the picture was taken between 1905-1910.

The final piece of importance to the eventual town was the arrival of Leonard Soper in Darlington. A year later he built a flour mill on part of Lot 9, Concession 1, purchased from Augustus Barber after whom the town's creek system was named initially. The eastern waterway would eventually be known as Soper Creek, by which several mills arose, including MacKay's—the latest version of which was built in 1905 and produced Cream of Barley. Today that building is occupied by the Visual Arts Centre. These four significant pieces of property, along with lots 12 and 10 continue to define the boundaries and layout of the town.[13]

In 1853 Bowmanville was incorporated as a village, but remained part of Darlington Township until five years later when it became a town.[14] Thus began its period of political independence. Ironically, in its political realignment within the new ward boundaries of Clarington proposed in 1996, Bowmanville returned to a position of political submergence within what had once been Darlington Township.

As residents of Bowmanville looked forward in the 1850s a period of growth, prosperity, and unlimited ambition lay ahead.

Notes

[1] Squair, *The Townships of Darlington and Clarke*, p.43.

[2] Hamlyn, Lunney, and Morrison, *Bowmanville: A Retrospect*. (Bowmanville Centennial Committee, 1958), p. 1.

[3] "It may be appropriate to note here that, of these three families, it was the Burks who were most closely associated with the development of what we now know as Bowmanville." From Hamlyn, Lunney and Morrison, *Bowmanville: A Retrospect*, p. 1.

[4] *Historical Atlas of Northumberland and Durham Counties.* (H. Belden and Co. 1878), p. 44.

[5] Squair, *The Townships of Darlington and Clarke*, p. 53.

[6] Hamlyn, Lunney and Morrison, *Bowmanville: A Retrospect*, p. 5.

[7] Squair, *The Townships of Darlington and Clarke*, p. 56.

[8] Fairbairn, *History and Reminiscences of Bowmanville*, p. 39.

[9] Hamlyn, Lunney and Morrison, *Bowmanville: A Retrospect*, p. 5.

[10] Heritage Walking Tour of Historic Bowmanville, *The Belvedere. (Quarterly Journal of the Bowmanville Museum)* No. 1. (Bowmanville Museum: 1993), p. 14.

[11] "...we need not be too embarrassed when visitors to our town express surprise at our eccentric street system; the old section of the city of Boston has much this type of thing and Bostonians tend to regard it with a touch of civic pride..." from Hamlyn, Lunney and Morrison, *Bowmanville: A Retrospect*, pp. 4-5.

[12] Squair, *The Townships of Darlington and Clarke*, p. 53.

[13] Ibid, pp. 43-44.

[14] *Two Centuries of Change: United Counties of Northumberland and Durham 1767-1967.* (Cobourg: 1967), p. 27.

Chapter Five

Our Bank

*"The study of history can be very therapeutic, it's far better
than the couch."*
– Harvey Dyck, discoverer of Mennonite Archives in the Ukraine

J ohn Simpson began his working career as a young clerk in Charles Bowman's
small store in Darlington Mills. The enterprise gave credit allowing new pio-
neers to survive and a grateful community took Bowman's name. It was an
important lesson for young Simpson. Hence, in 1856 when he was approached
by Montreal businessmen connected with the Montreal City and District
Savings Bank who were proposing a bank for Bowmanville, he agreed. In 1857
Simpson became the first president of the chartered Ontario Bank with a capital of $400,000.[1]

It was a bank that would support small merchants and farmers whose credit
was several times better than the amount requested, but whose occasional
shortfalls were annoying to traditional bankers. Simpson hated these ogres of
finance and hoped to drive out their ultimate practitioner, the Bank of
Montreal, for whom he had been local manager.

Simpson, a liberal within a Conservative company, was not adverse to using
the bank to forward his own political interests. He was free in dispensing loans
from the new bank sometimes to men with little credit but much influence in
the game of politics. One of his "shopping" trips, however, landed a large lumber group who added their accounts to the bank.

Such matters, however, were perhaps part of the bank's successful camouflage
of its real power which lay in Montreal among its more significant investors.
These included sixteen Québec patrons owning more than one hundred and
twenty-five shares as against only five investors in Bowmanville, three from
Oshawa and one from Whitby. Nevertheless, the myth of Bowmanville's
supremacy in the new bank continued for many years. Farmers had more
confidence in an institution whose directors were visible on local streets.
According to Leo Johnson, "So concerned were the shareholders of the Ontario
Bank that it appear as a local enterprise, that in the first twenty years of its existence (while its head office was in Bowmanville) it was never admitted in public that the bank was controlled from Montreal. It was always referred to in the
local press as Our Bank."[2]

This image was powerful enough to imbue the small town with the kind of
prestige and glory which could attract and support other business enterprises.

What has been described as "the most beautiful commercial building in Bowmanville", and which no longer exists—the Ontario Bank building—which stood on the north side of King Street, just west of Temperance. This picture dates back to circa 1910.

Bowmanville had every reason to believe that it was on its way to becoming a major centre in Ontario. After all, it was about the same distance to Toronto as Hamilton was in the west.

The Bank continued to grow by supporting new branches in other centres which locally included Whitby, Oshawa, Port Hope, Port Perry and Lindsay, and more distantly but perhaps importantly, Montreal. In 1869 the owners attempted to move the bank's headquarters to Toronto, a much larger centre with better financial prospects, but the merchants and farmers of Bowmanville and area still held some influence and power. The head office remained in Bowmanville for another five years.

As glorious as this brief history was, it reflected the behind the scenes reality of Bowmanville's loss of urban fortune to Toronto and its failure to establish a regional prowess. Some minor form, however, was recognized by the beautiful bank building constructed in 1866 which should have remained a community symbol forever. Eventually, the Ontario Bank did relocate to Toronto. In 1882 Alexander Fisher, brother of David who built the house that eventually became the Bowmanville Museum, blew his brains out after realizing that the money he had embezzled for friends and relatives abroad had been discovered. Then, in 1890 Rolly Moffat, accountant in the Toronto branch and an investor in the Toronto Baseball Club was found to have directed significant bank dollars to Chicago stocks. He would serve several years in the Kingston Pen and then leave the country.

By 1906 the bank had invested heavily in speculative stocks to restore previous losses, at least partially the result of embezzled dollars. The bank sank deeply into debt, in a manner similar to the contemporary disaster that befell Barings Bank in Britain in the 1990s. Finally, the Ontario Bank collapsed and its assets were assumed by the very institution Simpson had fled, the Bank of Montreal.

Until then folks in Bowmanville might have wondered why so much of their local capital invested in the bank failed to resurface in community initiatives. Now they knew it had always been redirected to the majority interest in Montreal. From now on they could at least be certain that their profits and investment would reside in the Québec city.

John Simpson's legacy, however, continues to this day. His son, D. Burke Simpson, spent time in a New York sanatorium for the treatment of tuberculosis, but he survived to become a prominent local lawyer with provincial and national connections. His accomplishments included attendance at a meeting in 1890 at which the Ontario Hockey Association, the precursor for all later hockey organizations, was formed.[3] When he died, his law practice was assumed by a young lawyer from Perth, Ontario, W. Ross Strike, who later became chairman of Ontario Hydro. He passed his firm on to his son, Al, who in the 1990s was joined by his own sons.

Notes

[1] Much of the information in this chapter is derived from The Belvedere (*Quarterly Journal of the Bowmanville Museum*) No. 3. (Bowmanville Museum:1990).

[2] Leo Johnson, *History of the County of Ontario 1615-1875*, pp. 248-249.

[3] Scott Young, *100 Years of Dropping the Puck: The Story of the OHA*. (Toronto: McClelland and Stewart, 1989), p. 14.

Chapter Six

Genuine Original Men are Scarce

"Bowmanville made excellent liquor and its citizens consumed it at alarming rates."
– Shane Peacock, *The Great Farini*

"...we are nursing a viper in our midst which is stinging our very vitals."
– *The Canadian Statesman*, 29 April 1869

Winter was, in many ways, a more pleasant experience in the 19th century. In the absence of snow plows, salting machines and sophisticated central heating, the only response was a grudging acceptance.

Nothing better symbolized this than the sport of curling. Near Vanstone Mill and south of the bridge carrying the Kingston Road, two of Bowmanville's first curling pads flanked a skating rink. By 1877 a shed protected curlers from the harsher elements of the season, but it had no heating nor could the rinks be protected from January thaws. Still the rink site was covered with six inches of clay and thoroughly padded to ensure that the eventual sheet of ice was firm and lasting.

In January 1869 Colonel Frederick Cubitt and William Roaf Climie were teammates on Bowmanville's number three rink against Orono.[1] As well they partnered for the married men (invariably dubbed the Benedicts in reference to Shakespeare's confirmed bachelor who is deceived into marriage) in their competition with the town's single men. In the cold and fraternity of play they shared and, in their way, created the atmosphere for town life and identity. Bowmanville was no longer an anonymous location on the planet, but a defined place which people called home and defended with pride when away.

What made the curlers real people, however, rather than the antique cliches of small town friendship, was the intense rivalry which often exploded into public anger and even hate between messieurs Climie and Cubitt. These two men in many ways symbolize the vitality of Bowmanville life in the last century, when its citizens could believe that they were the centre of the universe and its newspaper could proclaim itself *The Canadian Statesman* and not earn snickers for pompous overreach.

Who were these two men who could encompass so much of the life of their town and in turn define its meaning for their fellow citizens?

In late November of 1872 an Indian was brought before the magistrate's

23

MAYORS: 1858-1900

James McFeeters 1858—1859 &1861

Frederick Cubitt 1860 &1866—1874 & 1879

George Haines 1862—1865

Francis McArthur 1875 & 1880—1883

William Thompson 1876—1878

Robert R. Loscombe 1884—1885 & 1893—1900

Six 19th century Bowmanville mayors.

Bowmanville Messenger,

AND DURHAM AND NORTHUMBERLAND WEEKLY COMMERCIAL ADVERTIZER.

OPEN TO ALL PARTIES. INFLUENCED BY NONE.

V.   BOWMANVILLE, FEBRUARY 7, 1855.   No. 12.

The first known newspaper in Bowmanville was the Messenger. It was published as early as 1850.

The Canadian Statesman.

DEVOTED TO POLITICS, ART, SCIENCE, AGRICULTURE, LITERATURE, TEMPERANCE AND EDUCATION.

THE EXPEDIENCY OF PRINCIPLE IN OPPOSITION TO THE PRINCIPLE OF EXPEDIENCY.

VOL. II   BOWMANVILLE, C. W., THURSDAY MORNING, JANUARY 8, 1857   No. 21.

The Bowmanville Messenger was purchased in 1855 by the Reverend John R. Climie, a Congregationalist Minister. He renamed the paper, "Canadian Statesman" that year. The weekly was sold by Reverend Climie to his son, Reverend William Climie in the early 1860's, after a few years of joint proprietorship with him.

Canadian Statesman.

VOL. XIX.   BOWMANVILLE, ONT., THURSDAY, JANUARY 29, 1874.   NO. 22.

William R. Climie was editor and publisher of the Canadian Statesman until 1878 when he sold out to Moses A. James. The James surname is still on the masthead.

Reverend William R. Climie.

Moses A. James.

William Climie, Bowmanville's original "Statesman" and his successor Moses James.

court proceeded over by Colonel Cubitt, the Mayor of Bowmanville. By this time the only remnant native population in the area, never large in number, had lost any sense of the independence that the first European arrivals had encountered. The nameless aboriginal brought before Cubitt's court was a scarred figure found drunk in a public place and fined three dollars. No action was taken against the whiskey salesman "...although the law in some places will put an individual six months in a chain gang who sells whiskey to an Indian". [2]

William Climie was furious and mocked Cubitt, commenting, "...the tender hearted mayor inflicts in this case no punishment." Climie's medium was his newspaper, *The Canadian Statesman*, which he had assumed from his father, John, a Congregationalist minister. Climie and Cubitt's disdain for each other, more pronounced by the likelihood of almost daily encounter in this town of a few thousand residents, reflected their backgrounds and public philosophies.

Cubitt was among the early English arrivals in the fledgling town. His father, Woolmer Richard Cubitt MD, a graduate of Edinburgh University in 1823, had been the owner of a large estate, Erpingham, in Norfolk. Formal records show that he married Mary Churchill and had three sons, Richard, Fleetwood and Frederick. Curiously Squair's history says, "There was also, probably, a son John Churchill..." and leaves it at that. [3] They came to Darlington Township in 1833 and, just four years later, eighteen year old Frederick had a life changing experience as a volunteer with the Militia force that marched to Toronto to confront the rebel forces of William Lyon MacKenzie. It would forever confirm him as, what Fairbairn called, a Conservative dyed in the wool. [4] It began as well a lifetime association with the military which saw him rise to the rank of Lieutenant-Colonel of the 45th Battalion.

The Cubitts, however, were more than defenders of the Family Compact which controlled the political affairs and much of the province's best land. They liked to entertain, they drank and they may even have been somewhat the playboys of the western world. Of the three sons, Doctor Richard was described by Fairbairn as "...a great favourite with his acquaintances; he was very sociable and friendly. They kept bachelors' hall at the mill and I have been told, led a right jolly life." [5]

The Climies, on the other hand, were profoundly, though progressively, religious, noted teetotallers and proponents of the temperance movement. John Climie was a leader in the Congregationalist Church with its cultured and progressive mandate. He came to Bowmanville sometime around 1848 to assume the pastorship of the church, established locally at least as early as 1840. He purchased a local newspaper, *The Messenger*, and in the mid 1850s (sources conflict as to whether it was 1854 or 1855) brought out the first issue of *The Canadian Statesman*. [6] It was a name full of pomp and ceremony but also civic responsibility, signifying that even a small community played a major role in the national territory that only became a country in 1867. Over the past century and a half Bowmanville and *The Canadian Statesman* have become synonymous. We might say, fairly, that Bowmanville is *The Canadian Statesman* and it would be hard to imagine the town without the independent-minded journal.

John Climie's son, William Roaf, was born in Simcoe County in 1839 and thus had no experience of the Upper Canada Rebellion, but he would not escape its impact. Congregationalists were one of the few denominations associated with the insurgents though this was as much due to their espousal of religious tolerance and education reforms as to any actual support. Years later William Climie would say, "William Lyon MacKenzie was an extreme man; had he not taken the stand he did we might still be under the iron heel of the family compact. Who can imagine the condition of society of the present day had these men not been sterling patriots."[7]

The Climies were devoted to reform, but on one issue they tolerated no backsliding. Alcohol was a scourge. It was cheap, plentiful and seemingly everywhere. It destroyed families and the culture of violence in the mid 19th century could be laid at its door.

Climie's own paper, suspect only because of its owner's point of view, spoke of numerous tragedies. James Borland was shot in the face by his brother, thinking he was a cat committing depredations near the barn.[8] In 1868, "A farmer by the name of John Cotter was shot dead at the door of his brother-in-law, a farmer named John Gay, by the discharge of a gun. He had drunk liquor shortly before at the station hotel of the Grand Trunk Railway."[9]

And in the same year, "Ladies cannot come home from church on Sunday evenings without being jostled against by low blackguards that congregate at the various corners on King Street. Well dressed, well paid street rowdies are allowed to collect at corners and make use of their vile language before passing ladies without fear of interruption."[10]

Vulgar behaviour, however, was not solely the result of excessive drink. It represented an extreme occurrence in a more open society akin perhaps to that of the late 20th century—a world either to be feared or fully joined. In the remaining decades of the 19th century it would gradually be replaced by that of a more closed society of conventions and restrictions on social behaviour, which has become the prevailing image of the Victorian era. We can look at these two protagonists and conclude that Colonel Cubitt was a guardian, though from a life of privilege, of the open world and Mr. Climie, aware of its excesses, a proponent of a more closed and safer world.

As far as William Climie was concerned the fault lay at the feet of "...too many public men who fear the enmity of rum lovers and shrink from opposing the curse and cowardly submit to the wishes of the dispensers of the stuff".[11]

Significant among those, of course, was Frederick Cubitt, a man not inclined

Train coming into the Grand Trunk Railway Station circa 1910.

to long-winded diatribes or philosophical musings unless they could assist his political allies. He was foremost a man of action as never better illustrated in his service to Canada's first Prime Minister, John A. Macdonald, on his appearance in town at an election rally in September 1867, two months after the new country's genesis. Macdonald, a Conservative, wanted to follow his Liberal counterpart, George Brown, and neither man would budge in their desire to speak last.

The *Globe* reported that Macdonald's friend, "Cubitts [sic] rose and attempted to speak against time. The uproar and calls for the premier became so great that Mr. Cubitts was unheard, but so long as the time of the meeting was frittered away Mr. Cubitts purpose and the Premier's was answered....so when Cubitts became tired of gesticulating, hat in hand he took a hearty laugh at the fun of the affair."[12] In frustration Brown finally took the podium so Macdonald's purpose was served.

The hearty laugh reveals the real Cubitt. In his youth he played for the renowned Darlington Cricket Club. In the 1840s and 50s this team became the most visible symbol of the area's evolution from an almost accidental stopping-off point on the way to somewhere else, to an intentional community in which pride of place was celebrated in the fortunes of a sports team. Cubitt's teammates included T.C. Sutton and St. John Hutcheson, his fellow worshippers at St. John's Anglican Church—notable for its continuing receipt of an endowment provided by clergy reserve funds a hundred years after the Rebellion fought to end this excess of the Family Compact.[13] This team played urban representatives from Cobourg in the east and Toronto in the west, though they shared a similar social background.

Mr. Climie was also a sportsman. He had an interest in baseball, a game connected to America from which also emanated those ideas favouring more liberal forms of representative government, educational opportunity and freedom of religion. Mark Twain said that baseball represented the spirit of the 19th century. But for Climie his respect for the frivolousness of games was tempered by the needs of his society. He attended the Great Reform Convention held in Toronto in 1867 and expressed his philosophy bluntly through his paper.

"A man may be born," he said, "grow up, pass through life, and die in a place, and yet that place never receives one particle of benefit from his existence. He might as well have never lived. A turnip or a cabbage would exert just as favourable an influence on the public mind as he does. ...Genuine original men are scarce. ...One can conceive what a place would be if entirely controlled by such men—a Sleepy Hollow kind of paradise. ...It is the duty men owe to themselves and their fellow men to encourage a liberal public spirit."[14]

So the climate was set for their rivalry and it testifies to the arrival of Bowmanville as a distinct place that men could invest such struggle with so much meaning.

Their rivalry begins with their different politics, their family backgrounds and even the different bat and ball games they played. It received its ultimate impetus however from their respective positions in this new community. From 1866 to 1874 Frederick Cubitt was Bowmanville's mayor while William Climie published the town's leading newspaper. Though separated in age by twenty years they were, nevertheless, both at the peak of their emotional, physical and public powers. The collision, like those occasionally reported in that century between trains on the same track, was inevitable.

It's not clear where it started. The elements were all there, but this was after all a small town. People met on a regular basis. They shared a common interest in their community's welfare. They socialized and played outdoor curling in conditions that would bind even apparent enemies.

In his role as the town's magistrate, Cubitt dispensed justice for matters involving vagrancy, drunkenness, using abusive language on the highway, obstructing streets, using blasphemous language and causing a disturbance on a public street.[15] Liquor was often involved in these offenses and the colonel was often seen to take a tolerant position. On this one issue Climie would accept no backsliding. The mayor's nearly eight years in office were drawing evermore ire from *The Canadian Statesman* which viewed him as not only soft on the liquor issue, but also in Climie's words, "...a faithful paymaster to himself" and a man who could not match the challenger F. F. McArthur in appealing to the town's business interests.[16]

Bowmanville's fortunes had been on an upward spiral. By 1867 the town was said to be in a period of modest prosperity. "The harvest has been plentiful and the trade of the neighbourhood is…in a flourishing condition….This is a turning point in the history of Bowmanville. It is the flow of the tide which, as Shakespeare says, leads on to fortune. We have some good public buildings. The new Ontario Bank is an ornament of the town. We want an increased number of private dwellings of like respectability and comfort."[17] The town's public infrastructure including sidewalks and roads, however, was in need of significant improvement, most particularly Liberty Street which "…was not safe enough to walk along in the day time and certainly not at night."[18]

Through the 1870s the town entertained grand notions such as a railway from Bowmanville to Georgian Bay[19] and another to Bobcaygeon by way of Lindsay.[20] Both would allow the hinterland regions to take advantage of Bowmanville's Port Darlington Harbour and its access to American markets particularly for the shipment of grain. In 1873 F.F. McArthur, manager of the Upper Canada Furniture Company, reported a large increase in his business over the previous year. The decade also marked the arrival of the Dominion Organ and Piano Factory which by the end of the century had a world wide reputation.

The growth might have been even greater but for the decision of a carriage maker in the village of Enniskillen, about eight miles north of Bowmanville on the 8th concession. Every year Robert McLaughlin brought his cutters and carriages to the Bowmanville Fair. In 1873 a severe depression followed a financial panic in the United States. Many banks went out of business and with them the credit required by large and small companies. Grain prices were depressed and merchants were unable to collect debts. No one was buying carriages and McLaughlin survived by retrofitting existing wagons and repairing anything that customers brought him.

Known in Bowmanville as the country carriage-maker, his workmanship was respected, but his location made for costly deliveries and a limited local market. After the death of his wife, Mary, in 1877 and a second marriage within a year, McLaughlin decided to move to a larger centre. He might have chosen Bowmanville which was certainly the family choice. His brother, Dr. James McLaughlin, a prominent Liberal, owned the Rathskamory House and estate (which is now the Lions Centre on Beech Avenue) in the town.

According to Heather Robertson,[21] Robert chose to go to Oshawa because he did not want to live in his brother's shadow and because, if anything, Bowmanville was too successful. The town had six carriage makers to Oshawa's one. As well Bowmanville's Ontario Bank was Conservative and Methodist, whereas McLaughlin preferred Oshawa's Dominion Bank owned by Liberal Presbyterians and a smaller bank, the Western, which was prepared to loan him money. The decision to go to a community nine miles closer to Toronto would

One of the first automobiles in Bowmanville—a ten cylinder, fire engine red McLaughlin Touring Car with brass trim. Purchased June 12, 1908. Owner Fred Foster is driving. His wife Mabel is seated beside him. Daughter Doris is closest to camera in the back seat. The other family members are unidentified.

change forever the fortunes of the two towns, as McLaughlin's business eventually became General Motors of Canada.

This climate of business growth and its attendant economic cycles of decline created tremendous unease in a community struggling for supremacy in a region recently carved out of a wilderness. There were only limited forms of public and private welfare or other supports for people whose businesses went bankrupt or who were thrown out of work.

So following the business crisis of 1873 one can only imagine the added impact of a free-spirited religious movement which appeared in Bowmanville, preaching women's liberation and free love. Aberrant behaviour was not looked on kindly by *The Statesman*. Stories had appeared warning of terrible doings in the rural lands north of Bowmanville. In reference to the Township of Cartwright it was noted that it was "…a region of darkness, superstition and rowdiness… many instances of which I could repeat such as belief in ghosts, witchcraft, signs etc….I have sold packs of cards and books of vulgar songs to the youth." [22]

Spiritualism, however, was a powerful and organized threat. At its root is the belief that spirits of the dead can and do communicate with the living. At an intellectual level it developed out of a spiritual and mystic resurgence based on the writings of Emanuel Swedenborg, Rosicrucianism, along with North American Indian Shamanism and spiritism. Its practice included trances, clairvoyance and communicating with spirits by rappings. Significantly, women and men are viewed as equals. A future Canadian prime minister, Mackenzie King, was the sect's most famous adherent. The belief in a more liberal lifestyle and religious experimentation suggest a variant of what we now might associate with New Age beliefs.

Its fiercest international opponent was Charles Darwin who generally kept a low public profile, feeling he had created enough trauma in his time with his evolutionary theories. Yet he could not be dissuaded from confrontation because three of his own children had died at young ages and he loathed what he called "clever rogues" who deceived and exploited bereaved families. His allies included the eminent biologist, Thomas Huxley, and Huxley's assistant, Edwin Lankester, who later, as head of Britain's Natural History Museum, ironically accepted a fake fossil known as the Piltdown Man as the real thing.

Mr. Darwin and Huxley's allies in the small communities of Empire however were often men with far less noble intentions. The case was put best by Climie's newspaper in September 1874. "The more that is known of Spiritualism, as judged by the utterances of its leading advocates, the more disgusting and debasing does it appear. Advocates call for the destruction of the Christian religion, the repudiation of the generally accepted inspired teachings of the bible, and the obliteration of the marriage laws. Men and women shall be free to select at will those with whom they might desire to mate. Males and females should be freed from all legal restraint in matrimonial matters, and placed on a level with the beasts of the field. Hon. Warren Chase who recently lectured in this town and advocated the "social equality" longed for by the sisters. Well may those free lovers wish for the overthrow of religion and the destruction of the bible. God's word is the great obstacle in the way of the spread of their infidel licentiousness."[23] There were allegations as well of sorcery, enchantment, divination, magic, necromancy and witchcraft.

An even more vigorous opponent was the Reverend Cephas Barker of the Bible Christian Church, whose weekly religious paper, *The Observer*, was a rival to *The Statesman* for advertising dollars. It upheld a strict morality on even the most innocent of activities.

In 1873 Barker had launched a stinging attack on the Wesleyans, particularly their socials "…lotteries, election cakes with gold rings in them, some of the worst passions aroused in them, gambling, dancing, quadrilles, ladies in the lowest of low top dresses at them, ladies pressed and squeezed by young men going to them, of the passions aroused you have no wish to speak…"[24]

Presumably, all the prominent businessmen of Bowmanville posing in front of Frank Pethick's barber shop, now 26 King Street West. The date is about 1910. The picture was taken for the Bell Telephone Company to point out its first office location in town. It was in the rear of this premises between circa 1880 and 1882.

The election of 1874 was bound to be a close affair. Climie lined up on the side of McArthur, the candidate of the town's manufacturing and commercial interests who perhaps unfairly blamed the economic woes of the day on the incumbent Mayor Cubitt. Climie's paper also carried allegations that Cubitt was dipping into the town's finances and those of St. John's Church.

Cubitt was a fighter and he allied himself rather surprisingly with the rigid Mr. Barker who continued to attack everyone including Cubitt's own "English" church. Still politics makes for strange bedfellows.

Climie responded by linking Cubitt with the tavern keepers who feared the increasing power of the temperance movement (by 1891 at the opening of the high school it was reported that not one tavern remained in town). Cubitt played his trump card linking McArthur's campaign with the free lovers of the spiritualist movement.[25] This charge, however, was somewhat muted by Cubitt's own declaration that "...he had seen his grandmother three nights in succession—that he had been troubled by a nightmare—that instead of sitting on the mayor's chair he imagined it was on his head, and a gigantic burden was crushing him to the earth." [26]

Finally this ugly little campaign descended to ethnic slurs with Cubitt's forces suggesting that "…Mr. Cubitt should be elected because he is an Englishman and Mr. McArthur a Scotchman." [27] Climie was forced to repeat his observation of several years before that, "There were parties who openly declared they would not vote for a Scotchman. What are the causes for this morbid hatred of the Scotch we are at a loss to divine; but Scotch habits, Scotch recreations, are the continuing butt of these meddling malcontents…nor that we should profit much by…strong lunged long tongued crack brained fanatics, hysterical women damning dervishes." [28]

Voters went to the polls on the first Monday of 1875. One elector was caught voting for Cubitt in both the north and south wards "…while the gallant Colonel early in the day helped to swell his own list by voting for himself—a course not pursued by his opponent." [29] At day's end McArthur had outpolled Cubitt 249 to 218. In the south ward, home to many who had burned him in effigy a few years before, R.R. Loscombe was returned as a local councillor.

For Cubitt it was the second blow in the space of half a year. Earlier in July he complained that Major Smith had been appointed to a position above him in the 45th Battalion. Cubitt claimed that "…if staff appointments are made by selection not by seniority it will disorganize the whole volunteer force." [30] I might not be the best, Cubitt implied, but I've been around the longest.

The ex-mayor did not take his departure from office gracefully, however, declaring himself both a Christian and a gentleman, and alluding to misdeeds on council. Climie responded sarcastically, "The people appeared much surprised, still they tried to believe him because he repeated it a great many times, but as they belonged to the common herd, most of them grits and heathens, they didn't know he was either a Christian or a gentleman." [31]

In response to Cubitt's concerns that publicans were having trouble getting their liquor licences, Climie responded that a temperance mayor (McArthur) was obviously too much for the former mayor and that people had heard that well known sound "I Frederick" so often they could tell it from afar. [32]

Both men confronted each other regularly at school board meetings and not surprisingly their healthy dislike for each other eventually led to "blows." In early September the two men became embroiled in a procedural argument. Climie flared at Cubitt calling him a blackguard.

Cubitt later responded that, "Mr. Climie persisted in referring to me by name … I strongly object to my name being used by a person of so disreputable character, or by a blackguard." [33]

Cubitt grabbed an ink bottle and threw it in the general direction of the newspaper editor. Climie damned it a cowardly and disreputable act and police magistrate, George Haines, himself a former mayor (1862-65), was called. At a court hearing a short time later Cubitt was fined $5 for the offense and though not, in those days, an inconsiderable amount, the greater dishonour was the public shame. His distress was exacerbated by the loss of his brown and white spotted hound which regularly sat by him every Sunday in church.

Climie called Cubitt's act a cowardly feat and said the "...colonel seems to delight in the occupation of a scandalmonger—having no other visible means of support—he may pursue the path in which he delights to tread and we shall take good care of the numerous skeletons in his cupboard." The secret of the colonel's biliousness Climie said, "...was Cubitt's claim that because he was a conservative he thinks he is persecuted. And further because he is a Conservative he made a fool of himself at the school board."[34]

Cubitt mocked *The Statesman* editor for pursuing the matter. "This editor", Cubitt said, "has been slinging ink at everybody else for years, only he doesn't sling it bottled up. Mr. Haines activated by political hatred has exaggerated and magnified a slight indiscretion into an assault."[35] Cubitt claimed he had no intent of inflicting injury but in a boyish, almost friendly manner threw the bottle toward Climie. Climie easily dodged the object and, Cubitt says, "It fell so gently it didn't even break. No one was hurt."[36]

"Against tradesman, mechanic, working man or poor man unfortunate enough to be brought before his worship, penalties are rigorously enforced for comparatively trifling offenses such as mine," concluded Cubitt.

Climie commented that everyone in the Dominion knew that Cubitt had a strange way of doing things. "To which of the classes listed by Mr Cubitt, does he belong. He is not a tradesman, he has too much blueblood for that. He is not a mechanic, for he could not construct a wheelbarrow. No one here ever accused him of being a working man, therefore he must be a poor man."[37]

A frosty silence characterized their meetings on the curling rink and each sought examples of the other's perfidiousness. That wasn't too difficult. As a license inspector it was Climie's duty to collect fees from hotel keepers. In one instance a defendant paid Climie a minimum fine to avoid the costs of calling witnesses, but later and at Cubitt's instigation, wanted his money back because he didn't realize the seriousness of the charges. Justice Haines said the evidence proved Climie had obtained money by unlawful misrepresentation "...but I cannot believe he did so with intent to defraud" and the charges were dropped.[38]

In another incident Cubitt claimed Climie had double billed the school board for a printing bill. Climie said the mistake occurred because a school board member, Cowle, paid the $20 bill in cash unbeknownst to the Board, then died. The Board unknowingly authorized a second payment.

In disgust at Cubitt's attacks, Climie launched his most vicious response. "Frederick Cubitt being an idler in the common acceptance of the term faithfully serves his master in the work congenial for idle hands to do. Locally it is well known that he is continually plotting against political opponents who stand in the way of his exaltation, and in nearly every case where trouble arises from false charges against reformers remove the covering and you will find the Cubitt grub at the root of the mischief." [39]

For his part Cubitt claimed that Climie allowed advertisements in his paper for lewd purposes, low jokes and slanderous articles concerning Mr. Cubitt. Referring to his early days at *The Statesman*, Cubitt reminded townsfolk that Climie had slandered the Honourable Mr. John Simpson and in 1865 had called his future ally, Mayor Haines, "…an uneducated, prejudiced, incompetent magistrate either too ignorant or too stupid to fill up even a simple form of conviction."

"Climie has done his best to vilify, scandalize, injure or annoy others," Cubitt claimed, "I never read the *Statesman* but if only a small part is true, then in the estimation of Climie, Mr. Cubitt must be a personage of importance. Not even Sir John A. Macdonald has filled so large a space in the *Statesman*, and received so much abuse, slander and lies." [40] In conclusion Cubitt cited Samuel Johnson's reference to a journalist famous for his libels. "Change the name to Climie," Cubitt said, "and the application is perfect. Lying and slander are to him as the breath of his nostrils; they are the fetid pabulum with which he nourishes the morbid vitality of a pestiferous print." [41]

Climie responded by calling Cubitt an idler in the common acceptance of the term, "It is a well known fact that he is a drone on society, without visible means of support, caring only for his own aggrandizement and elevation to office, no matter at whose expense or what the means used to effect his object. Today he is degraded and despised, and let him chew the cud of reflection." [42]

By the end of the decade while still a relatively young man in his early forties, Climie began to withdraw from his public role. First to go was his beloved Bowmanville Royal Oaks ball club which had entered the top ranks of semi pro ball teams in Ontario. Next he sold *The Statesman* in 1878 to Moses James in whose family it has remained. Climie was perhaps quietly disgusted but satisfied in 1880 to observe the resignation and departure of his other rival, Reverend Barker, who had amassed a deficit of $55,000 for his church and paper. [43] Cubitt meanwhile returned for one more term as mayor in 1879.

A few years later Climie tried to return to the newspaper game, but *The Statesman* documented his mad rages in public when advertising revenues weren't forthcoming for his new paper, *The Sun*. He charged James with running the paper purely as a money-making enterprise and *The Statesman* "…frankly admitted the charge." Climie said *The Statesman* appealed to the Liberal party, for subscriptions. In their defense, *The Statesman* attacked Climie for attempting "…to rob us of the business you sold us to enable you to "square up" with your long-suffering creditors." [44]

Climie's *Sun* survived barely on the strength of his enthusiasm, but its future was tenuous. On 17 December 1890 a ceremony for the new high school was held. Over a hundred years later Bowmanville High School remains one of the most significant public institutions in town though it has moved from its original Queen Street site to the present location on Liberty Street North. Prominent graduates include world renowned concert pianist Ray Dudley (1944-1947); Nellie Lyle Pattinson, author of what became the annual Canadian Cookbook (1896-1900); and famous World War Two burn surgeon Ross Tilley (1918-1922) for whom a public school has been named in Bowmanville. J.B. Fairbairn observed "…that there was not a more moral or intelligent people in the Dominion of Canada. There was an intellectual status that was not about many other places of the same size in the province."[45]

The two old warriors were both there. A toast to the old boys of the area was given by Colonel Cubitt, "…but the Col., whose sight is failing, couldn't see the final 's' and somewhat reluctantly proposed "The Old Boy". Then a call for the press to respond brought the only representative of the fifth estate, W.R. Climie, to his feet with an appropriate speech. It was all in good spirit and humorously Edward Blake, the grand yet failed character of 19th century Canadian politics, proposed a toast to "the old girls."[46]

There was no sign of animosity between the old rivals of Bowmanville, both being in physical decline. In the summer of 1894 a provincial election brought charges that the Conservative candidate, Mr. W.H. Reid, "…did treat and drink whiskey with men of this town," as part of his election campaign.[47]

At the Liberal party's meeting the candidate W.T. Lockhart applauded the observation that the agricultural industry was five times as important as the next most important industry. On a more sombre note the meeting also referred "…in respectful terms to the death of W.R. Climie, who for many years had done valiant service in the Liberal ranks in West Durham".[48]

Climie had died from a combination of influenza and an abscess in the head producing paralysis of vocal organs and limbs. The funeral at his home "Sunrise" next to the present day St. Paul's Church was conducted with Masonic honours. Climie was referred to in biblical terms. "…there were points in Mr. Climie's character in which he resembled Elijah, and from which we could learn lessons beneficial to our lives. Like Elijah he took his stand for God and the right; like him he had warning of his approaching departure; and like him, he had, through the later years of his life, tried to make the most of every opportunity of serving God."[49] It was noted that Edward Blake was an intimate friend.

If it were possible for people to turn in their graves, Climie would undoubtedly have done so within weeks as the Conservative candidate Reid, despite his resort to alcoholic bribes, was elected to the provincial legislature. Even *The Statesman* with its fiercely Liberal heritage, noted, "What is more natural than that our Conservative friends should jubilate over their success. Over 50 years have they marked their ballots for naught. Old vets hugged each other in

Today's *Statesman* offices in Bowmanville.

delight—to enervating strains of the Dominion Organ and Piano Company, prancing steeds, bicycles, and vehicles ranging from Glover's four in hand hack to the latest style of McLung's Irish gig."

"Orators did orate and the old market buildings sent back again and again the echoes. They came in order, Mr. James McFeeters and Colonel Frederick Cubitt, two of the slain heroes of former political contests. Hillier, Prower and Loscombe chose not to speak." [50]

In 1897 the High School Board recorded "…the great loss it has suffered in the removal by death of its former member, the late Colonel Frederick Cubitt." [51] Cubitt had given forty years of service and was credited with the two magnificent school buildings the town now has"—one of which, Central Public School, provides education in the same, though expanded, building today. The colonel was described as a close personal friend of Sir John A. Macdonald.

"Like Sheridan the late Colonel Cubitt has left his character behind him… Kindness and sweet consideration for everyone seemed to be the greater part of himself. He always had a comforting and encouraging word for those who were striving to mount upwards on life's way, but a crushing sentence for all forms of ignominy or deceit." [52] As he had been at Climie's funeral, D. Burke Simpson was one of the pallbearers.

The deaths of Climie and Cubitt marked the end of an era in which Bowmanville citizens believed without doubt that their role was central to the affairs of the new Dominion. Time would erode this belief as locals fixed their gaze on their own boundaries recognizing the futility of influencing a nation's fate.

As for Climie and Cubitt, they are buried within a good inkbottle toss of each other in the Bowmanville Cemetery, all the better to pursue their rivalry into eternity.

Notes

1 *The Canadian Statesman*, 21 January 1869.
2 *The Canadian Statesman*, 28 November 1872.
3 John Squair, *The Townships of Darlington and Clarke*, pp. 118-119.
4 J.B Fairbairn, *History and Reminiscences of Bowmanville*, p.10.
5 Fairbairn, p. 10.
6 Squair, pp. 313-314.
7 *The Canadian Statesman*, 15 April 1875.
8 *The Canadian Statesman*, 27 March 1873.
9 *The Canadian Statesman*, 22 October 1868.
10 *The Canadian Statesman*, 10 September 1868.
11 *The Canadian Statesman*, 16 April 1868.
12 *The Globe*, 5 September 1867.
13 Hamlyn, Lunney and Morrison, *Bowmanville: A Retrospect*, p. 60.
14 *The Canadian Statesman*, 16 April 1868.
15 From *The Canadian Statesman*, 4 August 1870, "WARNING TO BOYS - Two boys were arrested and placed in the lock-up last night, for having stolen fruit from some gardens in town. On being brought before the Mayor, they were discharged, with a caution that if again found guilty of a like offence they would be severely punished. Boys, keep out of the gardens, or Coleman [the police chief] will be after you."
16 *The Canadian Statesman*, 2 January 1875.
17 *The Canadian Statesman*, 24 November 1867.
18 *The Canadian Statesman*, 24 November 1867.
19 *The Canadian Statesman*, 11 December 1873.
20 *The Canadian Statesman*, 4 May 1871.
21 Heather Robertson, *Driving Force: The McLaughlin Family and the Age of the Car*. (Toronto: McClelland and Stewart, 1996).
22 *The Canadian Statesman*, 6 August 1868.
23 *The Canadian Statesman*, 17 September 1874.
24 *The Canadian Statesman*, 17 April 1873.
25 *The Canadian Statesman*, 7 January 1875.
26 *The Canadian Statesman*, 10 December 1874.

27 *The Canadian Statesman*, 10 December 1874.

28 *The Canadian Statesman*, 13 January 1870.

29 *The Canadian Statesman*, 7 January 1875.

30 *The Canadian Statesman*, 2 July 1874.

31 *The Canadian Statesman*, 25 March 1875.

32 Ibid

33 *The Canadian Statesman*, 23 September 1875.

34 *The Canadian Statesman*, 30 September 1875.

35 *The Bowmanville Merchant*, 1 October 1875.

36 Ibid

37 Ibid

38 *The Canadian Statesman*, 2 May 1878.

39 Ibid

40 Ibid

41 Ibid

42 Ibid

43 Hamlyn, Lunney and Morrison, *Bowmanville: A Retrospect*, p. 55.

44 *The Canadian Statesman*, 18 July 1884.

45 *The Belvedere (Quarterly Journal of the Bowmanville Museum)*, Spring 1990.

46 Ibid

47 *The Canadian Statesman*, 20 June 1894.

48 *The Canadian Statesman*, 13 June 1894.

49 *The Canadian Statesman*, 20 June 1894.

50 *The Canadian Statesman*, 4 July 1894.

51 *The Canadian Statesman*, 10 November 1897.

52 *The Canadian Statesman*, 10 November 1897.

Chapter Seven

Places of Grace

*"The old fashioned stage coach, with its "shrill echoing horn",
was still the chief mode of travel. It was clumsy and slow,
but jolly."*

– James Young, Public Men and Public Life in Canada

*"The Italian countryside is never just landscape or nature
trails, never just a stroll, but full of roadside gods, reminders,
little idols, so that you can hardly take your children out of
the house here without discussing religion, life, death and,
above all, miracles."*

– Andrea Lee, New York Times Review of Books

*"The excitement attendant upon the Riel Rebellion in the
Northwest had just subsided and the next best tonic to inflate
public interest was a bangup good baseball match."*

– from the Guelph Mercury, 1886

*"Men are delicate as roses in winter and need to be wrapped
in warmth or else we die... as for women, they can't take over
the world fast enough for me. They should take over business
and government and manage society and finance and let guys
be artists and hoboes."*

– Garrison Keillor, Book of Guys

What makes the story of the 19th century so appealing is its oddity in contrast to our own time; the wild buffalo that roamed in the early days of the settlers and gave their name to a short-lived community north of Bowmanville near Tyrone; the odd occupations of cobblers, wheelwrights and wagon makers; the cricket team that was Bowmanville's first great sporting "franchise"; and, before the train first reached Bowmanville in 1856, the horse and carriage arriving along the Kingston Road with post horn blowing and Alphonso Hindes' dog howling, signalling the arrival of mail and illegal passengers who the driver had allowed to "jump the pole".[1]

We hardly understand the remnants of that time that survive and yet so directly effect our own in ways only distantly grasped. Signs of an older Bowmanville, for instance, can still be found in openly public places such as the large stone step bearing the name of "King" which sits on the lawn near the south end of Beech Avenue. William C. King, the town Postmaster, who died in 1921, owned the large house on the corner and also built the double house

41

next door. This was a gift to his newlywed daughter who lived on one side and received income through rental of the other half.

Around the corner on the Lowe Street sidewalk is the fading, indented name of "Kent" marking the family home of Bowmanville postmasters, Carl and son John, who followed King.

There are messages as well in buildings such as St. John's Anglican Church. A small memorial plaque in the church is dedicated to Edward Pethick, a sergeant in the British 59th Regiment Foot. It harkens back to a period of the British Empire when Bowmanville was a minor crossroads, and records Pethick's service under the Duke of Wellington, the hero of the Battle of Waterloo. Pethick is buried beside St. John's church in what once had been an important cemetery.

Above the alter of St. John's Anglican Church is the stained glass vision of William Holman Hunt's "The Light of the World", originally painted long after the inspiring influence of the pre-Raphaelites had run their course in 19th century England. The painting of Jesus with lantern in hand knocking at a door, hangs in St. Paul's Cathedral and toured Canada, New Zealand and Australia in 1904-05. For many it became a symbol of Victorian sentimentality and memories of being dragged to church. To Doctor Solomon Cartwright Hillier, Bowmanville's Mayor from 1913 to 1915, it was a powerful symbol of his age. Like many men of his generation Hillier cared about symbols. His distinctive and wonderful home at the corner of Beech and Lowe was intended to be a "...great improvement to the Avenue" with its modern heating and water facilities.[2] After his death his family dedicated the reproduction of the Hunt painting in stained glass form to the church.

Elsewhere in the same church there is a tall stained glass window dedicated to the memory of Allan Napier Macnab, the eldest son of the rector Reverend Alexander Macnab who practised in Bowmanville from his induction in 1853 till his death in 1891. The Macnabs were of the famous Clan Macnab of Scotland. Their ancestral home was known as Dundurn. It was the name given by one of the Macnab family to their home in Hamilton, Ontario. Today it is an important historical site in that city. Of only somewhat less prominence, but still a remarkable property, was Alexander Macnab's residence on Bowmanville's Concession Street. The Dundurn name was also used here and remains etched on the sidewalk to this day.

Alexander's eldest son, Allan was born in Cobourg in 1848 where his father was practising then. Of the boy it was said, "...he seemed never to have lost the grace of baptism."[3]

He followed in his father's ecclesiastical path graduating from Trinity College in Toronto with a Bachelor's degree in 1869, and then, afflicted by the beginning of what appears to have been continuing depression and mental instability, he was forced to leave school and study under his father's direction, eventually being ordained as a deacon in 1871. He immediately began studying for Priest's Orders, but suffered a complete nervous breakdown on the day of his examination and withdrew.

"He repaired at once to Bowmanville when it was hoped that country air and exercise ... would soon have a favourable influence upon his health."[4] His father had left for Europe in the fall of 1872 and young Allan attempted to replace him at the parish of St. John's, but it was with little success. Hearing of his son's depressed condition, his father made arrangements for Allan to meet him on the continent.

In Montreal, however, the young twenty-four year old, recuperating it was said from a sun stroke, jumped into the river near the Victoria Bridge and drowned. It was later said that he was frightened by several locals running towards him after they observed his odd behaviour.[5] There's little doubt that Allan killed himself, but no one could bring themselves to admit such a catastrophic conclusion and in most accounts it was referred to as a death at sea.

He was a victim of his age and perhaps of a certain madness brought on by too much religion. He could not escape his failures or perhaps a sense that his own beliefs and commitment were not as fierce as his own father. Perhaps in another time he would have been a school teacher, or even a minister in an age when this profession was not so prominent.

There was darkness in the 19th century and for most people it outlived their short time on earth. Poor Allan was not so fortunate. Nor was a miller in nearby Hampton whose fate demonstrated a culture of violence and free access to guns with which our own age would tremble.

In September 1874, W.G. Vanstone, a respectable man of the village of Hampton a few miles west of Tyrone in which the Vanstone family owned a local mill, visited Henry Elliott's grist mill also in Hampton. Here he played with an old Enfield rifle and teased the young son of the resident miller, Isaac Moynes. "Should I shoot your father?" he asked. Moynes had only time to say, "Why you would not have your pa shot would you?" when the gun fired and instantly killed Moynes.[6] The coroner warned of the need for care in the handling of dangerous weapons and the affair drifted into history, while in 1886 the Vanstone family purchased the Bowmanville mill with which their name is still associated.

The casualness of gun play was again demonstrated in late August 1874 when a pop man's dog was stolen from outside the Alma Hotel. The hotel's owner, Thomas Shaw, upon investigating was shot and wounded. The accused, William Watson, with his counsel St. John Hutcheson, was brought before Mayor Cubitt but the hearing was postponed because the pop man had left town.[7]

Not all, however, was tragedy and remorse. Games were the glue that allowed the community to feel its unity and express that in competition with nearby places. Yet even these had features which we in the late 20th century find odd.

Bowmanville's council chamber was filled on the evening of 11 June 1868 as the friends of bat and ball games met to re-organize their town's cricket and baseball teams. Frederick Cubitt was elected president of the cricket club with William R. Climie, his vice-president.[8] A committee was appointed to sod the bowling crease on the ground adjacent to the Drill Shed recently constructed in the north end of town (on present day Carlisle Avenue) in response to the Fenian troubles. Two years before a band of Irish sympathizers had landed at Hull's Marsh as part of a larger strategy to strike at British interests in North America.

Officers were then selected for the Live Oak Baseball Club which played on the grounds north of a factory on Thursday and Saturdays at 6 p.m. Climie was appointed president, supported by Benjamin Werry as vice-president and Samuel Burden, the secretary-treasurer. The popularity of the two bat and ball games in 19th century Bowmanville and their future was a story repeated throughout the Dominion.

The fate of cricket and baseball was inevitably tied up in the changing nature of Ontario society. The Colonel's game of cricket had much in its early favour. Youth from around Ontario, educated at Upper Canada College and themselves members of the colony's conservative ruling class, brought the game back to their small towns where they in turn assumed leading positions as members of the judiciary, local government, the medical profession etc. Cricket was their informal means of maintaining the social cohesion of a local ruling class as well as providing opportunities to meet with the elite of Upper Canada. On 8 June 1846 Charles Neville, Secretary of the Darlington Cricket Club (composed of players from Bowmanville and the surrounding Township of Darlington) invited the Cobourg Club to play a friendly match in Bowmanville on the 17th. In the absence of either rail or adequate roads in what was still a pioneering community, the Cobourg players travelled by stagecoach and the steamer "America."[9]

Bowmanville's cricket ground was located on a park like setting just north of the then settled part of town in an area bound by present Lowe Street, Beech Avenue and Centre St. Deer roamed the top end where it was still wooded.[10] Here in 1852, fourteen year Bill Hunt who became world famous as the tightrope walker "The Great Farini", mounted his first show, a children's circus, on the open cricket pitch.[11]

In this idyllic setting Bowmanville beat Cobourg by twenty-four runs. A month later on 18 July, as recorded in Hall and McCulloch's *Sixty Years of Canadian Cricket*,[12] the visit was reciprocated. John Bailey, an unordained preacher of the Methodist Episcopal Church in Bowmanville, scored 10 and 36 in his two at bats (players bat in both of cricket's two innings). It might have been more except that a heavy shower between innings caused Bailey to tumble head first on his wicket. The umpires could not decide whether he was out or not. Both sides agreed to await the verdict of the Toronto Cricket Club which later ruled against Bailey. Twenty subsequent runs were deducted though Darlington still won the match.

Darlington's other notable batsman was Thomas C. Sutton. Sutton was an ideal representative of his class. He was a shareholder in the Port Darlington Harbour Company, a church warden at St. John's Anglican Church in Bowmanville, a future Quarter Master of the Third Battalion of Durham and a municipal councillor in 1853. Sutton was recognized as an outstanding under-hand bowler and a stiff "bat" who played on many select provincial teams against Upper Canada College.

The Toronto Globe recorded additional matches by the Darlington club in 1848, and Hall and McCulloch described a 16 September 1852 match in Toronto in which the bowling of Sutton and Cubitt was "...dead straight at the wicket...in them Darlington had a pair of excellent bowlers."[13] Darlington's leading batters were Sutton and John H. Holmes, a lieutenant alongside Cubitt and Sutton in the Third Battalion. The lineup of their Toronto rivals included J.O. Heward, J. Helliwell, C.J. Rykert, Dexter, Madison and George Barber, all of whom had or would shortly have international playing experience.

By the time of Darlington's match in Toronto on 11 July 1855, the Bowmanville based team had been together for at least ten years, a considerable period of organizational success, but not surprising given the elite membership of the team. They counted on public support though it was mostly symbolic in contrast to that extended by politicians to sports teams in the 20th century in the form of taxpayer funded stadiums. The Governor General Sir Francis Bond Head, and Lady Head attended the 1855 match and *The Globe's* reporter hoped not only that the cricketers would prove "...the efficacy of physical training in assisting mental requirements",[14] but that more women could now attend following Lady Head's example "...for the modern cricketer puts forth his best energies by the consciousness that bright eyes look upon his efforts."[15]

The Darlington Club retained its exclusive membership at the time of the 1855 match in Toronto. It marked the first reference to St. John Hutcheson, an Upper Canada graduate, splendid fellow, club secretary, and a prominent Bowmanville lawyer. The club's president Frederick Cubitt was into his second decade of play. These Darlington cricketers played intersquad games or matches against other towns whose lineups conformed to their social class. They had little interest in proselytizing the game's merits to the general public, which in Darlington consisted of about 8,000 people in the one hundred and fifteen square mile township.

In 1857, however, despite good showings against Toronto and Whitby, *The Canadian Cricketer's Guide* reported that "...the strength of the Darlington club is necessarily weakened by the recent establishment of two other clubs in town—the "Franklin" and the "Union."[16] At this point the trail of bat and ball games in Bowmanville grows cold for a decade. This is a period of startling change in the fortunes of cricket and baseball.

Whatever momentum cricket had as a better organized and better played bat and ball game was forever forestalled by the American Civil War. This internal conflict among other things caused the suspension of the incredibly popular and almost annual international series between Canada and the United States.

As for baseball, John Squair who was born in Bowmanville in 1850 says that "...so far as I remember we did not, during my early youth, play base-ball or foot-ball" but more informal bat and ball games such as one and two old cat were common as well as crude games of shinny.[17] Baseball's strongest centres in Canada in the 1850s were in the area west of Toronto. Vacationing Americans who crossed Lake Ontario by boat from Rochester introduced baseball into Cobourg in the 1860s. From there the game spread throughout the Counties of Northumberland and Durham, the jurisdiction within which Bowmanville was located.

It is likely that baseball had been played in Bowmanville for at least a few years before 1868, given *The Statesman's* reference that year to the apparent reformation of the "old" Live Oaks. At a Dominion Day celebration they defeated a factory team from the Upper Canada Furniture Company 49-9.[18] Later in the day that same Factory club lost by only a run to a team of players from the surrounding Darlington Township.

In August, the Bowmanville Sons of Temperance Nine, including Ben Werry, William Climie, a local school teacher Malcolm McTavish, and members of the McMurtry and Burden families defeated a picked nine from town whose members included Tom Shaw.[19] These individuals would not only be important in baseball's growth in the 1870s, but represented a different set of values from those of the early generation of cricketers, being either small business men or middle class professionals.

Newcastle and Bowmanville played a spirited series in early October of 1868, won by the Beavers.[20] A year later a juvenile squad, the Victorias, was formed in Bowmanville.[21] That same year a third major summer sport, lacrosse, was organized in town with the local team travelling to Rochester.[22] In August, Captain Bill's lacrosse club from the Six Nations "...dressed in costumes of varied and fantastic appearance and ornamented with feathers, paint and other decorations peculiar to the red men" visited Bowmanville.[23]

In 1870 with time running out on cricket's prominent place in the summer sporting calendar, an attempt was made to re-establish the game in the town under the chairmanship of lawyer, Robert Armour, a victim of the real estate collapse in 1857. Frederick Cubitt was club president and the team included two baseball players, Climie and Samuel Burden. Merchants were requested to let their clerks play during the week and hope was expressed that Bowmanville would "...regain its old position on the cricket roles."[24] The best bat and ball skills, however, were now found among baseball players. When cricketers were challenged to a game of baseball against the local team they were allowed to have three extra men on the field.[25] Ballplayers invested time and discipline in maintaining their game's prominence. A year later Climie, batting third for the Live Oak Baseball team, noted in his newspaper that "beautiful muffings give evidence of want of practise.(sic)"[26]

In 1872 *The Statesman* reported, "There having been no cricket ground in Bowmanville for a number of years, the noble game is almost unknown here now."[27] Some new arrivals in town organized a series of matches with Whitby, but by now cricket had become a kind of warm up or practice session for a majority of players whose first game was baseball. These included David Fisher, Climie, Burden, Thomas Shaw, R. McConochie and W.J. McMurtry.

At a fireman's picnic at the Drill Shed grounds in Bowmanville in that 1872 summer, teams from Hamilton, Cobourg, Oshawa, Port Hope, Lindsay, Napanee, Port Perry, and Belleville competed in a variety of competitions from baseball to bands.[28] In mid August, Bowmanville's junior squad, the Victorias, played the second nine of the Toronto Dauntless Club. The Victorias' train arrived in Toronto around 10 a.m. and, after touring the town, the players were feted at the Caer Howell House where the match was played on the cricket ground. Samuel Burden from Bowmanville umpired the match which the visitors won 32-30. The result was telegraphed back to Bowmanville and a large crowd gathered at the train station to welcome them home.[29]

In 1873 the best team in Canada and one of the top ten in North America, the Guelph Maple Leafs, visited Bowmanville. They won easily 25-2 and the local paper called it the most correct display of ball play ever witnessed in the town. "They knew their business and played well together. Evidence is given of what practise and judgement will do," said Climie in *The Statesman*.[30] Baseball, with its absence of social custom and social ties, matched the ethos of the emerging business class who respected hard work, serious effort and skill more than entrenched privilege.

Later that season spectators paid 15 cents, and a half holiday was declared for the 2 p.m. Friday game against the St. Lawrence of Kingston, whose lineup included five American professionals, including a raucous battery of Rafferty and Dygert. *The Statesman* said that they were "...not fit for the society of respectable people—they are not wanted anywhere a second time, with their obscenity and profanity. Hotel keepers along the route do not want a second call from them, and at the railway station here one third of the party beat the bus driver out of his fare."[31] Kingston players berated the umpire every time a call went against them, but the quality of their play like that of the Maple Leafs was guaranteeing baseball its place as the leading sport in North America.

In the process the ability of small towns to compete with larger ones paying more money for better players gradually began to disappear. Before this happened, however, it was still possible for villages like Newcastle to receive an offer to play the best team in baseball. The Boston Red Stockings [who by dint of historical evolution are today's Atlanta Braves] were on tour through the American mid-west in the summer of 1873. Their manager and the future hall of famer Harry Wright telegraphed John Templeton of the Newcastle Beavers to see if he would be interested in a match. Templeton agreed to Wright's terms, but Boston accepted a better offer from Toronto and never made it to Newcastle.[32]

Baseball was confirmed as the leading sport in Bowmanville with the establishment of the Royal Oaks team in 1874, under the presidency of William Climie. This semi professional team allowed Bowmanville to enter the ranks of the best teams in Ontario and reminded the remaining cricket establishment in the community of their one time position in Ontario sport. The Fly Aways of New York were among those invited to play the Royal Oaks.[33]

The game's successful commercialization in Bowmanville benefited many local businesses. Thomas Shaw was not only a rather stout member of the team, but proprietor of the Alma Hotel where the players would eat and drink after the game. Billiard tables were found in most hotels and that popular sport was found guilty by association and condemned from the pulpit.[34]

The high point of the Royal Oaks 1874 season was the visit of the Guelph Maple Leafs on their way home from a tournament victory in Watertown, New York. Bowmanville lost 20-7, but the Guelph players said that they were the best Canadian team they had played that year.[35] Confirming that judgement, the Royal Oaks beat Kingston 13-10 in a game called after six innings so that Bowmanville could catch a boat back to their hometown. They were declared the champions of Eastern Ontario.[36]

Meanwhile locals heard about the unfriendly behaviour of the Young Ontarios Club of Bowmanville towards their rural cousins, the Eckfords of Orono. "We wish to complain of the ungentlemanly behaviour," an Orono resident complained. He told *The Statesman* that Bowmanville had sent an unpaid telegram in response to a paid one, had delayed the start of their game until dusk and then taken the field with two members of the Royal Oaks on their team. They had stolen the Eckfords game ball and refused to repay the previous favour of the Orono players who had treated Bowmanville to dinner on a visit to their village. At least the Eckfords won 43-27.[37]

By 1876 the best senior baseball in Ontario had divided into two levels. The top level teams from London, Guelph, Kingston, Hamilton and Toronto played in the new Canadian league, while the others continued to play in an informal circuit of arranged matches. Unlike cricket which had failed to attract wide-spread public support, baseball was by now rooted in the idle tossing of a ball between fathers and sons, attendance at community games and its simple play at school and workplace picnics and holiday gatherings.

The game found favour with a newly enfranchised majority of the population,

Four young rakes posing cockily with cigarettes. Captured in the bloom of youth, the confidence of a new century showing in their faces. This photo was taken in February 1901. Back row, Clarence Meath and Wallace Shaw. Front row, Alex Beith and Fred Downey.

but even its growth would reach limits that the public would find distasteful. Port Hope's visit to Bowmanville for a game with the Royal Oaks was marred by ungentlemanly street behaviour by Port Hope youths. Bowmanville's eastern neighbour had a reputation as a place in which, "The number of young men under the influence of liquor was lamentable, many of them too, of the better class of society." [38]

In mid August, the premier Canadian team, the London Tecumsehs, visited Bowmanville's Drill Shed grounds. [39] Their visit was the beginning of a last hurrah for Bowmanville's struggle to compete in bat and ball games with larger centres. What had begun with the Darlington Cricket Club was climaxing in the struggles of the Bowmanville Royal Oaks baseball team.

Baseball, like other sports, was slowly segregating towns into divisions of equal strength and commercial ability. It was no doubt a fair solution to the problem of competition, but it also served to reinforce the cultural and economic withdrawal of smaller towns from their once ferocious rivalry with places like Hamilton and Toronto. The Tecumsehs with two future National League stars, Fred Goldsmith and Joe Hornung, won the hard fought game and stayed afterwards for a strawberry social and sing-a-long. Such camaraderie and fraternalism also would disappear soon from the game.

The 1877 season brought Bowmanville to the forefront of Ontario baseball competition. London and Guelph had joined the American based International Association and the field was now open for teams competing for the Ontario championship which local papers persisted in calling the Canadian title, though no other provinces were represented. The team met in *The Statesman* offices in April and William Climie announced his intention to play a diminished role in the team's operation though his brother George continued to be involved as scorekeeper.[40]

The team's pitcher was Jim Schofield who worked in the Dominion Organ Factory on Temperance Street and was locally renowned as one of the early curve-ballers. "He gave in easily however," said one of his teammates, Ed Livingstone, "always complaining of a bruise or sore arm so he could not always be depended upon."[41] Edwin Coleman's diary described the opening of the local baseball season between the Royal Oaks and Ben Werry's Old Swamp Angel team. He described Werry as "…the hero of a hundred baseball scraps."[42] The Royal Oaks defeated Toronto and Markham early in the season, but the London Atlantics led by a future major league pitcher and umpire Bob Emslie easily beat the Oaks 19-0.[43]

Bowmanville lost a contest in Woodstock after walking off the field to protest an umpire's call that Coleman could only take one base after a wild throw past first.[44] Scandal soured the Hamilton Standards visit in August when Tom Shaw overheard two Hamilton players urging their manager to umpire that day's game because "This team [Bowmanville] is too heavy for us and we intend to squeal and you can help us." Squealing was a big part of Hamilton's game and they eventually forfeited it.[45] At season end *The New York Clipper* noted that Bowmanville had finished third in the Canadian championship.

The Royal Oaks were by now a commercial enterprise. Under the management of Jim Schofield season tickets were sold in 1878 and new players welcomed.[46] William Climie's withdrawal from the team at the same time as he was selling *The Statesman*, likely due to health reasons, deprived it of administrative support and the publicity afforded by the town's leading newspaper. The team lacked the ability to compete at a semi-professional level and soon disbanded.

The success of teams like the Royal Oaks, however, had made possible the game's penetration into the everyday lives of citizens in settings as diverse as amateur competition and family picnics. Its integration into the working life of common people was a symbol of the kind of society reformers like Climie cele-brated. By the 1880s baseball teams in Bowmanville represented the furniture factory, the organ factory, the merchants on the north side of King Street, millers, clerks and shoemakers.

The professionals who had played for the Royal Oaks found success in larger centres. Jim Wilcox was a local boy who first played baseball in Bowmanville as a fifteen year old in 1868 and, a decade later, played catcher for the Oaks with-out benefit of glove, mask or protector, but only a piece of protruding rubber between his teeth to prevent them from being knocked down his throat. After the team folded he went to Harriston, Ontario where he played for the profes-sional Brown Stockings alongside Bob Emslie. Wilcox went to the Cass Club of Detroit in the early 1880s making $150 for the season and later played in the American south before retiring in Cincinnati.[47]

As for cricket, it had become a game with no remaining connections to the everyday life of Ontarians. Even the visit of the great English cricketer, W.G. Grace, to Toronto in 1872 couldn't revive its fortunes. It served as a symbolic reminder for a few of a British past and had a specialized function as the prop-erty of only a social elite.

Sports in the 19th century was almost exclusively a domain for male activ-ity and so it is ironic that one of the few surviving pieces of that century's life was of a more gentle quality.

It was never intended to be such, but the Pelican Card Club, formed in Bowmanville in 1890 on King Street above Cawker's Butcher Shop, became a place of fragile beauty for older Bowmanville men. Some were widowers, some bachelors and others simply seeking male companionship.[48] It is interesting to note that a hundred years later this spot would be occupied by Leisure Lady Women's Shop.

This was a place where men could tell slightly risque jokes as was reflected in their poem on the walls,

> "A wise old bird is the Pelican
> Whose beak will hold more than his belly can
> He can hold in his beak enough fish for a week
> But I don't see how in the Helly can."[49]

One of the Pelican Club members, Lou R. Wood, an agent for International Harvester, later provided the club with access to offices in his implement shop. The club was thus named Wood's Senate in recognition of the group's keen dis-cussions on local, provincial and federal politics.

They stayed here from 1937 until 1949 and built a reputation celebrated by *The Toronto Telegram* in 1951 as "...the only town in Ontario with its own municipal senate", where "...the problems of the town are thrashed out heat-edly and violently over a game of euchre."[50]

When Lou Wood retired, the "senators" rented a room above the Maher Shoe Store on Main Street and became simply the "Senate Club" with its fifty plus members generally fifty to eighty-five years of age. Eventually their numbers declined and the formally vital conversations on religion and politics declined to more leisurely, harmless patter. The Senate died on its 100 birthday in the library where it had taken final residence. A last game of cards was played by Ken Hill, Pinkie Hubbard, Clare Goodman and Cloyd Morey.

The delicate flowers of time had lost a place of grace.

The Original "Senate" in the card room above Cawker's Butcher Shop. The photo was taken around 1890 and everyone is suitably dressed for the camera. Beginning first table on the left foreground (clockwise): Carl Kent, George Mason, Fred Kidd, Bill Perrin. Wearing cap – Richard Fishleigh. With cigar in left hand – Fred J. Manning. Back row, from left, beginning with man standing – Charles Blair, John B. Mitchell, William C. King, Charles Keith, William F. Allen, Arthur E. McLaughlin, Pete Garrett (with dog), Alan Williams (standing). Thomas Fairbairn. Man with beard looking at cards (in front of dog) Robert D. Davidson. At right front table, clockwise from left: – James Deyman, John Moorecraft.

Notes

[1] George Vice, *The Post Office and Early Development in Bowmanville*, (Bowmanville: self-published, 1993).

[2] *West Durham News*, 13 May 1887.

[3] *The Canadian Statesman*, 12 December 1872.

[4] Ibid

[5] Ibid

[6] *The Canadian Statesman*, 24 September 1874.

[7] *The Canadian Statesman*, 27 August 1874.

[8] *The Canadian Statesman*, 18 June 1868.

[9] Hamlyn, Lunney and Morrison, *Bowmanville: A Retrospect*, p. 6.

[10] William Bagnell, letter to *The Toronto Star*, 6 September 1988, p. 5.

[11] The Hunts lived around the corner in a house that still stands on Lovers Lane and were among the town's elite attending St. John's Anglican Church. Shane Peacock, *The Great Farini: The High-Wire Life of William Hunt*. (Toronto: Viking, 1995), p. 20.

[12] Hall and McCulloch, *Sixty Years of Canadian Cricket*. (Toronto: Bryant Printing, 1895) p.29.

[13] Ibid, p. 40

[14] *The Globe*, 16 July 1855.

[15] *The Globe*, 16 July 1855.

[16] *The Canadian Cricketer's Guide*. (1958).

[17] John Squair, *The Townships of Darlington and Clarke*, p. 349.

[18] *The Canadian Statesman*, 2 July 1868.

[19] *The Canadian Statesman*, 6 August 1868.

[20] *The Canadian Statesman*, 1, 8, & 15 October 1868.

[21] *The Canadian Statesman*, 15 July 1869.

[22] "Particulars regarding the excursion to Rochester...have been announced. The Norseman will leave Whitby at 4:30 a.m., Oshawa 5, Bowmanville 5:45, Newcastle 6:15, Port Hope 9:30, Cobourg 10 and will proceed to Charlotte direct, arriving there early in the afternoon.", 17 June 1869. (The same paper also contained details of a boys lacrosse club dubbed the "Erly Bird Laycros (sic) Club").

[23] "...the Six Nation Indians were also good and loyal subjects of Queen Victoria - three thousand of them being ready to take the field and fight for her Majesty should hostilities arise between Britain and the United States." *The Canadian Statesman*, 19 August 1869.

[24] *The Canadian Statesman*, 23 June 1870.

[25] *The Canadian Statesman*, 25 August 1870.

[26] *The Canadian Statesman*, 3 August 1871.

[27] *The Canadian Statesman*, 10 October 1872.

[28] "The streets were lined with people in all directions and it is estimated that from eight to ten thousand persons assembled to witness the demonstration." *The Canadian Statesman*, 12 September 1872.

[29] *The Canadian Statesman*, 22 August 1872.

[30] *The Canadian Statesman*, 31 July 1873.

[31] *The Canadian Statesman*, 14 August 1873.

[32] *The Canadian Statesman*, 4 September 1873.

[33] *The Canadian Statesman*, 6 August 1874.

[34] *The Canadian Statesman*, 5 March 1874.

[35] *The Canadian Statesman*, 16 July 1874.

[36] *The Canadian Statesman*, 24 September 1874.

[37] *The Canadian Statesman*, 24 September 1874.

[38] *The Merchant*, 26 May 1876.

[39] *The Canadian Statesman*, 17 August 1876.

[40] *The Canadian Statesman*, 19 April 1877.

[41] *The Canadian Statesman*, 28 September 1922.

[42] Excerpt from the diary of Edwin Chesterfield Coleman as found in the Bowmanville Museum.

[43] *The Canadian Statesman*, 12 July 1877.

[44] *The Canadian Statesman*, 9 August 1877.

[45] *The Canadian Statesman*, 16 August 1877.

[46] *The Canadian Statesman*, 11 April 1878.

[47] *The Canadian Statesman*, 31 August 1922.

[48] Much of the information on the "Senate" is taken from *The Belvedere* (*Quarterly Journal of the Bowmanville Museum*). No. 3 - 1990.

[49] Ibid

[50] *The Toronto Telegram*, 11 August 1951.

Chapter Eight

Not Afraid to Face Public Opinion

"Past acts or past traditions are not necessarily lost in time, because they can be recreated in the imagination."
– Peter Ackroyd, *English Music*

We know less than we would like of the lives of women in this age, their status being confined by a judicial and political system which treated them as less than full citizens. As late as 1928 the Supreme Court of Canada would declare women not to be "persons" who could hold public office as Canadian senators (a verdict reversed by the British Privy Council a year later).

We are left with glimpses, hints and odd tales which reveal much and suggest additional lines of enquiry. We need only examine the tragic though oddly fulfilling story of Charlotte Munson, a graduate of Toronto Normal School with a first class teacher's certificate, and a member of a respectable family. Engaged in teaching in Orono, five miles northeast of Bowmanville in 1864, she boarded at the home of James Kerr, a tavern keeper, "married and with three children."[1]

An intimacy, it was reported, sprang up between them. In early 1865, Miss Munson fled to Toronto where Kerr followed her. They met in a hotel where the teacher asked for the return of letters sent to Kerr. He not only refused "recognizing their power", but detained her in an adjoining room all night and told her he would make known all their transactions if she did not comply with his wishes.[2]

Shortly thereafter she and a friend, Miss Smith, took the train to Newtonville where they spent the night, travelled to Newcastle and hired a horse and buggy at Mr. Bradley's livery stables. They went north to Ballyduff and in the evening came to Watson's Hotel in Orono, where they sent for Mr. Kerr. He arrived, agreed to take them to Hampton, and consented to return the horse and buggy to Mr. Bradley.

They travelled back to the Kingston Road and through Bowmanville to the Scugog Road and then north along that road to the fourth concession. Miss Munson was reinforced by the laudanum consumed on the way—a headache remedy later advertised by leading department stores including Sears, but in fact a mixture containing opium.

Just after passing the toll-gate on the Scugog Road, Miss Munson shot Kerr and then attempted to kill herself. The gun misfired and Kerr first thinking he had been shot by someone on the road and them recognizing the shooter fled a mile and quarter down the road to W.H. Gaud's house from which he was

Ada Hind, one of the Salvation Army officers who helped established the Army in Bowmanville in 1884, and served as commanding officer in town during that year, 1885 and again for a period in 1886. She was also instrumental in organizing local efforts in aid of building the Army's temple on King Street East. Opened March 16, 1884, it was on the present day site of the Veltri Complex, east of Division. This portrait dates from the 1885 period.

conveyed to Brodie's Hotel in Bowmanville. " His case was pronounced hopeless and he lay at death's door." [3]

Locals could only conclude, that "...the unfortunate creature must be labouring under temporary insanity and driven to desperation through fear of her tormentor." [4] At the same time however this was also a woman attempting within the bounds of her society to take control of her life.

In examining the newspaper reports of the day one discovers heart breaking tales of a mother drowning her two children in Hampton and the grief stricken husband arriving home to the scene of mental anguish and struggling to understand the reasons and escape the fate of place and time.

A woman lived in a world of some madness, but life's spirit could also be evoked in the tender relations of men and women which ring with legitimacy and vitality even within the legal restraints of the era. No one captured this spirit better than the unnamed "Gossiper" whose columns were featured regularly in *The Statesman* through the summer of 1872. He was nastily dubbed "March Manyweathers" for his wide variety of opinion and though it is not certain he appears to have been Dr. King recently hired as high school headmaster by a committee chaired by Mr. Cubitt.[5]

The Merchant newspaper had refused on religious grounds to advertise travelling circuses whose operation and philosophy pointed to an age where men and women might perform or meet on somewhat equal grounds. The "Gossiper" betrayed a more open mind. "Unlike Cole's Circus which did not trouble to perform half of its announcements, Van Amburgh's Menagerie more than fulfilled the promises of its bills. The town looked quite lively and the itinerant showmen, cheap jacks, and such like appeared to be well patronised…"[6] and "The demoralization of the people of Bowmanville must indeed be something very terrible when in spite of all warning they will rush in crowds to listen to the lewd songs and obscene jokes of the circus ring and not only that but will actually come away and declare it was very good."[7]

On the contentious issue of women riding on horseback in the same manner as gentlemen, the "Gossiper" noted, "The papers will deplore the rapid strides towards masculinity, but I give honour to the five brave little New Yorkers who are not afraid to face public opinion…"[8]

On the matter of picnics and their social implications, he noted, "On Wednesday last there was an enjoyable picnic at a point a mile and a half east at which there was a very large and sociable gathering. There was dancing and cards and flirting to an unlimited extent by the light of the moon and kerosene lamps; and so I noticed several instances where the whisperings of 'soft nothings' into your partner's ear seemed to meet with a great deal of success."[9]

On a trip to Toronto by train carrying holidayers to the Grand Trunk Railway picnic, the "Gossiper" observed that "…in one seat was a young man between two girls, who seemed to vie with each other as to who would take the most care of him. And the cool way in which the lucky dog took their attention was quite refreshing. While one procured him water the other nestled his head upon her shoulder."[10]

The public rarely discussed sexuality, though newspapers like *The Statesman* in 1875 might advertise an essay for young men on a radical cure for seminal weakness or spermatorrhoea, induced by self-abuse or involuntary emissions and curable without resort to the knife. The paper would be sent in a plain envelope.[11] Young women were warned that Sir James Clarke's Celebrated Female Pill "should not be taken by females during the FIRST THREE MONTHS of pregnancy, as they are sure to bring on Miscarriage…"[12]—a not too subtle guide for those interested in an abortion.

Our most revealing glimpse of the curious relations of men and women and

An early (1907) casual photo of two Bowmanville women. Woman on left is Florence Mayer, girl friend of the photographer William Wesley Shaw who left town to work in New York City. She was daughter of a prominent Bowmanville furrier, Markus Mayer. The other woman is unknown.

that society's odd pursuit of justice was the case of one of Bowmanville's most prominent citizens.

Parties are often excessive affairs as was the celebration of the first anniversary of Canada's nationhood in Bowmanville. No arrangements had been made for a public demonstration on 1 July 1868. Even the ringing of the fire bell was delayed because no one showed up at the designated time.

The absence of organization was replaced by the imagination of local revellers. "Oppressed by the sun rays" they "...betook themselves to the taverns to get a glass of something to cool themselves. Feeling cooler another glass would be taken to warm them a bit. Idleness must be turned to some account and the Devil's most successful agent, strong drink, had the largest share to do in the celebration." [13]

William Climie, *The Statesman's* editor, blamed young lads from the surrounding countryside. They found the town's whiskey "...very elevating to ideas of personal courage and prowess and some disgraceful fights occurred at the taverns." [14] In other parts of town however celebrations in the summer of 1868 were traditionally marked by boating, swinging, quoiting, tenpins with a suspended ball, catching a greased pig competition, "...and music for those who wished to trip lightly on the greensward"[15]—the types of residual celebrations descended from the folk traditions of old England.

In the evening the primitive social bounds of the new community erupted. A man of prominent occupation, social position, and family background was publicly shamed though he had fled town several days before.[16]

Robert Russell Loscombe, barrister, was the "...son of the esteemed C.R. Loscombe—the Governor—who had brought his family to town while in the employment of the Grand Trunk Railway." Loscombe senior had taught eventually in a local and private classical academy, adopting principles of the famous Rugby Institute to enhance manly virtues through physical exercise. "He tried ...to make them gentlemen as well as scholars".[17] These were the days before legislated compulsory education when citizens purchased schooling, if they so chose, for their children.

The lawyer son, R.R., was the married father of six children, who "...contracted a rather strong affection for the maid of all work who reigned supreme in his kitchen."[18] In late June, Miss Grace Burt was spotted entering his office and citizens aware that Loscombe's "...conjugal relations for some time back have been sadly out of tune,"[19] speedily collected.

There was limited legal restraint to the behaviour of men like Loscombe. The citizenry relied on demonstrations of public humiliation dating back to the middle ages in which men, who had beaten or shamed their wives, were paraded through the streets on a donkey to the accompaniment of cowbells, clanging pots and derisive chanting.

Some of the Bowmanville crowd climbed to the roof of the building and through a skylight spotted the two together. The office was stormed but Miss Burt, could not be found. In the ensuing scuffle R.R. fled to his father's house. The respected "Governor" was "...severely bandied and cut"[20] while "...the lawyer left during the night for a distant portion of the Dominion."[21]

The July 1 holiday provided the perfect opportunity for public action. That evening, fuelled by alcohol, memory and European society's practice of folk retribution, they torched effigies of Robert Russell Loscombe and Miss Burt in the market square. It might not have been fireworks, but the message to the rest of the community was obvious.

A few years later in 1871, when matters had stilled and his successful legal career rebounded, Loscombe introduced a bylaw for the regulation of streets, sidewalks and thoroughfares. Included was a section for the preservation of order and suppression of nuisances.[22] His fear of the folk custom and action of his social inferiors was well founded.

And then nine years later the residents of Queen Street, east of Ontario Street, were relieved by the arrest of Ellen Downey, a tall, coarse featured, black haired woman of considerable physical development, age about 40 years, charged with maintaining a bawdy house: her legal defender—Mr. R.R. Loscombe.[23]

All of these details were reported by Mr. Climie's newspaper, *The Canadian Statesman*, fiercely liberal in its point of view and thus ill-disposed to the peccadilloes of noted conservative activists like Loscombe, who was both a future Mayor and pall bearer at the funeral of Mr. Climie's great rival, Colonel Cubitt.

Men never could sort out their attitudes about women's place in society, as if it were their duty to do so. Points of view ranged from patronising to progressive. Fairbairn's homily on the topic of race suicide, found in his 1906 Bowmanville history, warned of the consequences of Darlington's female population decaying through ill health in contrast to the virile and vigorous German "...or some other foreigner." [24]

His solution? "Our girls should be brought up to know that wifehood and motherhood are the two ideal states as ordained by the Almighty Creator..." [25] Fairbairn never considered that such sole pursuit may have been a contributor to the malady he described nor that such ideas spoke more to the need for social control than any realistic appraisal of the human condition.

Ladies Hockey Team (1924) represented Bowmanville in Lakeshore League. Front (l. to r.) Hattie Seymour Armstrong, Mildred Luxton Edmondson, Nell Piper Wilson. Back (l. to r.) Mansfield Cook, Maude Wilcox Elford, Bessie Kilgannon Donoghue, Alma Piper Cole, Nora Cluff, Gladys Mutton, Gordon Richards

Nina Neads became one of Bowmanville's first successful business women at a time when millinery and school teaching were among the few professional options available for women. She was one of the four children of Wilson and Elizabeth Neads. Nina's chosen field was insurance. She joined Harry Cann's insurance agency in 1911 remaining there until his death in 1916. A year later, she joined Edith Scobell's company, leaving in 1919 to start her own independent insurance agency which she maintained until her death in 1963. This photo was taken in the 1950s.

On the other hand *The Canadian Statesman* in 1922 warned young women against too early marriage. There were real burdens of married life as pointed out by *The Statesman*. "We have but one childhood and one youth, and which ever way we look upon it, married lives have their own responsibilities, which are very different from those which fill the lives of young girls."[26]

The article revealed a progressively disdainful attitude towards the commonly held belief in the romantic appeal of married life and female subservience. "How great is the hurt and disappointment when they discover their new home is seemingly empty and cold. Better for mothers to let their little daughters understand what they give up to make for such peace and happiness and let them see the real burdens of married life.

"When they are older, self-denial comes easier to them, they have more experience in troubles, hardships, and in doing without such things that in their school days they considered would be an utter impossibility."[27]

The glamour wears quickly off the "Mrs." title, *The Statesman* warned. Perhaps subconsciously supporting this, the paper covered the 1922 women's hockey season with special glee. In that year the Goodyear Ladies' Hockey Team lost 1-0 to the Thompson Knitting Team in the regular season, following a victory over the Ross Can Sextette. They then beat the Front Street Team

1-0 and advanced to the playoffs where they outscored Front Street again. The final was played on soft ice and went back and forth before Goodyear in their snappy blue and white uniforms beat Thompson 2-1 to win the Mason Cup donated by George Mason for the S.W. Mason and Son dry goods firm.

The banquet featured speeches, dinner and dancing by the young people in attendance. It was all very correct and pleasing, but above all symbolized the new role of young women in a society which had once ignored them but now at least could celebrate their performance on the ice.[28]

By the time that women were finally declared "persons" in the late 1920s, a few professions had provided opportunities for a career beyond the household. Schoolteaching was one obvious avenue and at any one time the majority of teachers at Bowmanville's oldest school, Central Public, have been female. A graduate of Central, Nina Neads, became one of Bowmanville's first successful businesswomen. She joined Harry Cann's insurance agency in 1911 remaining there until his death in 1916. A year later she joined Edith Scobell's company and left in 1919 to start her own independent agency which she maintained almost until her death in 1963. She was renowned for her knowledge of the large insurers and her ability to get the best deals.[29]

Notes

1. as first reported on 28 June 1865 and in several editions of *The Daily Globe*, Toronto.
2. Ibid
3. Ibid
4. Ibid
5. The Gossiper's free-spirited reign of opinion was attacked in early September when *The Canadian Statesman* (5 September 1872), no doubt reflecting W.R. Climie's point of view, condemned the anonymous scribe for his admitted "connection to the Conservative Party, the clog on the wheel of progress."
6. *The Canadian Statesman*, 25 July 1872.
7. *The Canadian Statesman*, 5 September 1872.
8. *The Canadian Statesman*, 15 August 1872.
9. *The Canadian Statesman*, 29 August 1872.
10. *The Canadian Statesman*, 29 August 1872.
11. *The Canadian Statesman*, 8 July 1875.
12. *The Canadian Statesman*, 15 July 1869.
13. *The Canadian Statesman*, 2 July 1868.
14. Ibid
15. *The Canadian Statesman*, 6 August 1868.
16. *The Canadian Statesman*, 2 July 1868.
17. J.B. Fairbairn, *History and Reminiscences of Bowmanville*, p. 58.
18. *The Canadian Statesman*, 2 July 1868.
19. Ibid
20. Ibid
21. Ibid
22. *The Canadian Statesman*, 3 August 1871.
23. *The Canadian Statesman*, 18 June 1880.
24. Fairbairn, p. 97.
25. Ibid
26. *The Canadian Statesman*, undated (early 1920s item).
27. Ibid
28. *The Canadian Statesman*, 22 March 1922.
29. Falls, Hobson and Humber, "A Centennial Celebration", *Central Public School 1889-1989*, p. 15.

Chapter Nine

A Drowsy State of Existence

*"I learned this at least by my experiment: that if one advances
confidently in the direction of his dreams, and endeavours to
live that life which he has imagined, he will meet with a success
unexpected in common hours."*
– Henry Thoreau, *Walden*

*"Dreams are particular things. They can be more real than
anything in the ordinary world. A dream brings out the secret
life of the world. It can reflect all the things we have forgotten
we knew. It can bring out the spirit of a place or a person, like
music which no one has previously been able to hear."*
– Peter Ackroyd, *English Music*

It is tempting to suggest that Bowmanville's growth in the late 20th century
owes much to the pluck and zeal of a local entrepreneurial class. In fact it
depends almost exclusively upon the community's gradual entanglement in the
greater Toronto region. This process had its first multiplier effect on places like
Mississauga and Brampton in the sixties, the southern portions of York Region
next, and slowly those towns east of Toronto.

In the hyperbole of sudden local achievement, the tendency has been to forget that it was the urban success of Toronto which created their new
economies. As oft as not, however, these nouveau riche both forget any debt
owed to the nearby city and in the process ignore the very process of mixed
urbanity out of which this wealth grew.

These attributed benefits of location make it easy to forget a time when prosperity was due to an ambitious local policy of industrial expansion in which the
competitive advantages of Toronto's proximity were less pronounced.
Bowmanville, Sher Leetooze observed in her local history of Darlington
Township, may appear at the height of its development today, "...but
Bowmanville's importance as a commercial and manufacturing centre has had
a decrease since its heyday in the early decade of this century." [1]

In fact the decline came even earlier than this. In the ten years between 1891
and 1901 Bowmanville saw its manufacturing plants decline from eighty-six to
ten. [2] No other statistic is required to detail the change in the town's position from
a forward looking aggressive place with faith in its future as a major centre, to an
inward-looking, self-absorbed place. Scott Little's 1978 essay on Cobourg, Ontario
described a fate shared by many Ontario small towns including Bowmanville.

Turn of the Century in Bowmanville (note the number of bicycles popular in the 1890s)

"The fifty year period between 1900 to 1950 was one of few significant occurrences in the appearance of the main street. A calm settled over many towns. Some fell into obscurity, but most crept along in some drowsy state of existence. The basic appearance of main street had been established and few major improvements that were not already initiated by 1900 took place. Paving of the main street was probably the most noted improvement."[3]

Perhaps the saddest spectacle of this lost golden age was the tale of the Dominion Organ and Piano Factory.[4] It began life in 1870 in Oshawa, manufacturing organs and melodeons. If location was everything than surely it should have remained there. The company moved however in 1873 to the corner of King and Scugog streets in Bowmanville. In that time it was a feasible proposition that Bowmanville had a more optimistic future than the community to the west. By 1879 the company had added pianos to its production. Now located in a new three storey, plus basement, factory at Temperance and Wellington, a grand future awaited.

It was a wonderful era for piano manufacturers. Ontario was now home to families that had been here several generations and who had collected the wealth necessary to invest in what we would call lifestyle products. With no contrivances of modern communications, a piano or organ was a profound consumer statement. The Dominion Company was led likewise by some magnificent personalities who combined private enterprise with public spirit. J.B. Mitchell was not only vice-president and superintendent , but also a mayor of Bowmanville. J.W. Alexander, the company President also donated land and a building for a town hospital. At the hospital's dedication in 1913 he urged, "...those who had wealth to remember such institutions as these and to do so while they were living when the satisfaction arising would be a rich reward."[5]

The reception afterwards at Dr. Hillier's "Ravenscraig" residence with its stone fence acting as boundaries to Beech and Lowe, revealed the way of life before the First World War. *The West Durham Review* described it as follows: "Some excellent addresses were delivered by the following gentlemen: Rev. W.N. Allin, Mr. R.M. Mitchell, and Mr. C. Wattleworth sang the madrigal from the "Mikado". The Goodyear Glee Club, under the direction of Mr. Wattleworth, sang some beautiful selections. Miss Florence Allin sang beautifully "For You Alone", and Mr. R.M. Mitchell received applause from the audience for the rendering of the old favourite, "I'll Sing Thee Songs of Araby". Mrs. Cawker and Mr. H. J. Knight sang in duet "Excelsior" which was well appreciated. Morrison's Goodyear Orchestra, Miss Shaw at the piano, played some lively airs during the evening to the delight of the audience. Mrs. W.B. Short took some $110. on a plate collection."[6]

The company was adventurous in pursuing new designs and using the latest mechanical ideas. It became so proficient in the use of wood products that, in the bicycle's great age of the late 19th century, the Dominion produced wooden bicycle rims. Internationally the piano and organ company had offices and representatives in Liverpool, England; Adelaide, Australia,; Johannesburg, South Africa; Dunedin, New Zealand; and Moscow, Russia. By 1916 its sales totalled over 80,000 instruments.

The company sponsored its own baseball team, as well as a company band. J.W. Alexander's son would later recall some of the two-hundred workers at the company during its peak, including, "Creeper—and Buzzy Furz, Mousy Morsehead, Jiggy Jeffrey and Wally Oak." He also remembered the sounds of the factory which would define for several generations their memories of Bowmanville. "The factory had a melodious whistle. It was one of the nicest factory whistles I've ever heard. We had a piano and organ company—I can understand that it was selected for that reason. You could hear it all over town; and you could also hear the sound of the cyclone sucking up the sawdust and shavings from the machines."[7]

The stock market crash in 1929, followed by a world-wide depression, in the thirties destroyed the market for pianos and organs. J.W. Alexander experimented with electronic organs and pianos, and produced the Mitchell gramophone. He diversified his corporate interests by investing in the Ross Can Company which had located in a new building (afterwards occupied by the Whiz Company manufacturing car polishes, and then in the 1990s by a flea market). He was friends of the Rehders who owned the local foundry and James Morden, operator of the Cream of Barley Mill.

All of his brilliance and public spirit however couldn't save the Dominion Organ and Piano Factory, possibly the greatest business Bowmanville will ever have. Others like the Goodyear Tire and Rubber Company of Akron, Ohio, have been more successful and survived longer, but their initial success was the product of a 35% import duty on American tires imposed by the Canadian government in 1909. Goodyear simply took over the Durham Rubber Company which in turn was descended from the Bowmanville Rubber Company founded in 1896.

J. W. Alexander believed in Bowmanville and his enterprise and it broke his heart in 1936 to declare bankruptcy. People just stopped buying the product. Besides the impact of the depression, entertainment could be obtained cheaply from the now popular radio. In 1938 the Alexanders left Bowmanville, and their house went to the mortgage broker. At the same time, part of the Dominion building was destroyed by fire. For Alexander it was the test of Job. The Specialty Paper Products Company occupied the building from 1949 to the building's destruction in 1990. Nothing remains but the odd organ and piano sold at auctions after its former owner has died.

Alexander's son told Dan Hoffman, "We investigated all avenues to see if we couldn't keep going—and we even thought of amalgamating with a casket manufacturing firm located in one of the towns north of Bowmanville. I remember my father saying, 'Ach—what a mournful business to be in' Pianos at least bring happiness and entertainment—and they're still doing it."[8]

Dominion Organ and Piano Factory Building, another lost Bowmanville treasure.

Goodyear Rubber Works.

In looking for signs of the end of an era in the social affairs of the town we return to February 1898. In the midst of his long reign as Mayor of Bowmanville (1884-85, 1893-1900) R.R. Loscombe invited members of Town Council, town officials, and friends to a banquet at his residence "The Elms." The Pethick Brothers and Messrs. Brown and Osborne rendered a choice program of music on mandolins and guitar.[9]

Mr. John Percy, chairman of the Finance Committee, then surprised the Mayor by reading an address to Mrs. R.R. Loscombe, mayoress of the town. His colleagues had left the cares and dimensions of municipal life and "...invaded the quietude of your happy and luxurious home—a home which for hospitality has a reputation as renowned and extended as the wealth and area of our vast Dominion." He continued, "...to you Dame Nature had been most lavish in her gifts. We at this time are much pleased to observe how lightly good old Father Time has touched your still beautiful brow, and from that observation we are led to believe 'That a charming woman never grows old'."[10] Then he presented her with a pair of chairs.

It was as if the past had never existed or that politeness and comfort had rendered it meaningless. And the description of the fine house and its well known estate-like presence as the "The Elms", suggests a fantasy world suspended outside the rigors of ambitious economic struggle and big city life—a world immortalized in literature by J.R.R. Tolkien in the mythical place of Lothlorien.

For in its decline was also the fruits of its survival. Bowmanville would become that magical, almost mystical place of small town lore. It would be no rival for

Staff of the hard tires department, Goodyear factory, Bowmanville, 1922. Left to right: George Raby, Ernie Jones, Lyall Burden, Charles Smith, unknown, Ben King, Joe Childs, E. Woodward, Harry Westnutt and foreman Alf Richards.

Toronto or even Oshawa which, with the grant of $50,000 in 1899 to the McLaughlin Factory, demonstrated not only the benefits of public investment, but also its prominence as the dominant urban centre of the region—a position Bowmanville might have claimed.

In the bargain, however, Bowmanville got something better—a small town perhaps, but one in which security, camaraderie and access to the countryside were readily available. It was a position that the town despite all kinds of changes and projections maintained a hundred years later.

Between 1881 and 1911 Bowmanville's population declined from 3504 to 2814 and in the last year of the 19th century welcomed a Canadian prime minister, Sir Wilfrid Laurier,[11] for the last time until John Diefenbaker passed through town. Nothing better symbolized the political irrelevance of what had once been a must stop for ambitious leaders.

Three thousand local citizens gathered at the Drill Shed grounds in what is now the area of Carlisle Avenue to hear Laurier. The Dominion Organ and Piano Company Band played "The Maple Leaf" and speeches filled the afternoon air. Union jacks and a picture of the Queen welcomed the country's leader.

By 1951 Bowmanville's population would rebound to number 5430 and that of Darlington Township would in the fifties finally regain the same total as it had one hundred years before. But the history of the town for the greater part of the 20th century is largely confined to businesses and personalities notable for their local import.

Notes

1 Sherrell Branton Leetooze, *The First 200 Years: A brief history of Darlington Township.* (Bowmanville: Lynn Michael-John Associates, 1994), p. 69.

2 Jacob Spelt, *Urban Development in South-Central Ontario.* (Toronto: McClelland and Stewart, 1972).

3 Scott Little, *Main Street - Cobourg, Ontario.* (Unpublished essay submitted in fulfilment of requirement for GGRC01Y at Scarborough College: University of Toronto), March 1978.

4 much of the information on the Dominion Organ and Piano Co. is derived from *The Belvedere (A Quarterly Publication of the Bowmanville Museum),* Summer 1988.

5 Ibid

6 *The West Durham Review,* — 1913.

7 *The Belvedere.*

8 Ibid

9 *The Canadian Statesman,* 16 February 1898.

10 Ibid

11 "The Dominion Organ and Piano Company Factory closed down for the afternoon so that the employees might have the opportunity of hearing and seeing one whose kindly face and graceful bearing won the hearts of all who heard his voice whatever their political views might be." Laurier's visit as reported 18 October 1899, in *The Canadian Statesman.*

Chapter Ten

The Lives of Ordinary People

"No doubt a child of eleven or twelve can accept all manner of strangeness before ordinary existence closes around him."
– Peter Ackroyd, English Music

"Each local place has its characters, upon whom the character of the place depends. Each place has people who have developed roles or businesses that are site-specific. Their skills and their habits are not geographically transferable. They might be able to move elsewhere and have the money to live for awhile, or even for a long time. But, emotionally, they would dry up inside. Many older people with money retire and move, only to discover too late that they are indigenous to their home town. Outside of that geographic radius life makes no sense."
– Jim Burklo, Whole Earth Review, Summer 1995

The lives of ordinary people are the real history of Bowmanville though of course ordinariness is a pejorative term which misses the reality and magic of all of our lives.

Stu Candler was born before the First World War. He was raised by his grandfather, Samuel Candler, the only one of the thirteen children of John Candler and his wife Ann Rhem to live his entire life in Bowmanville where he is buried. The Candler family, then consisting of two children had come to Canada in the late 1850s and lived on three acres of lot 21 on Darlington's Broken Front just west of Bowmanville. The property was the last place on the right hand side of Holt Road by the lake and was completely obliterated by the development of the Darlington Nuclear Generating Station.

According to family folklore they had left England after John's family had taken unkindly to his marriage to Ann, a serving maid.[1] The rift was so deep that John dropped the "h" in the family name of Chandler. In Bowmanville John and Ann eventually raised their thirteen children. John had no profession and the family survived by his acquiring pieces of work over an entire lifetime. His little property provided some essentials, but he worked at everything from ditch digging to hiring himself out by the day splitting rails, a job in which he cut trees for use as a farm fence. Given a choice between two men it was said that it didn't pay to hire John because he ate so much, but he was such a good worker he was hired anyway.

A majority of the family eventually moved to western Ontario in the 1880s, but the older children like Sam, born in 1859, remained in Bowmanville.

71

Central Public School in Bowmanville, built in 1889 and still in use today.

Another brother, William, born two years before Sam, left his wife and three children in Bowmanville some time around 1880 and didn't return for forty-six years. He broke a leg digging ditches in Detroit, but the wife of the man in the bed next to him discovered that he had played the trumpet on the streets of Bowmanville in the town's Salvation Army Band. She got William a job with Barnum and Bailey's circus band. He later played in John Philip Sousa's band.

Another brother, Edward, born in Bowmanville in 1876, worked on the railroads most of his life. He later told tales of working with a former member of Jesse James gang and running the train down the route of the legendary Casey Jones. Edward led a raucous life and family lore tells of his being mugged once while on his way from Wyoming to Bowmanville. He had drunk too much, gambled, and lost all his money and his watch. In later years he returned to Ontario to run a gas engine in a lumber shanty.

Lives such are these are quickly lost to history and it is time's fortune that Stu during his life became somewhat of a local amateur historian. He vividly recalled his school days at Central Public School beginning in 1915. "I had been ill all year but recall that Dick Widdicombe from Hampton took me to Central school that first year. Miss Scott was my first teacher and I had Greta Wickett in three grades. They kept promoting her to a higher grade each year that I passed. She had a violent temper. We used to goad her until she lost her temper and gave us the strap. But we just laughed at her. She couldn't hurt us.

"Miss Helen Morris taught grade six. She had no trouble with discipline as she would make us sing—that was a deterrent mightier than the strap.

Central Public School and Bowmanville High School. Stu Candler's two schools. The High School is now located in a modern building on Liberty Street.

"Miss Minnie Jennings was a real old maid—prim and proper. She didn't believe in the strap. Her favourite past-time when angry was to throw chalk at us. We'd try to catch it and throw it back at her. She really was a dear old soul. She always taught grade seven. I also recall Miss Amy McCowan who had been a missionary in China and told us the most interesting stories.

"Our principal R.D. Davidson was a strict disciplinarian. Looking back I believe we all liked him as we always called him Mr. Davidson even when speaking of him behind his back. I can't recall that we ever gave him a nickname."

"He generally visited each class at least once a week. In the lower grades he held a pin over the teacher's desk, and asked all of us to be very quiet as he wanted to be able to hear a pin drop on the desk top.

"Whenever the school yard looked dirty with lots of paper, Mr. Davidson would have all the boys stand shoulder to shoulder the full length of the school-yard and walk slowly across the yard picking up the paper scraps. He made a game out of the cleanup and we all liked it as we always had an extra long recess.

"I never saw him with a hat on, he always wore a cap.

"Mr. Laughlin was there for just a year after Mr. Davidson's health broke down. Next came Mr. Trussler. I think he was there for two years. His favourite past-time was to slap your face hard enough to knock you off your feet. One day he slapped the wrong pupil, Ken Caverley, whose father was on the school board. Trussler was gone at the end of the term.

"The last principal I had was J.H. Johnston. I liked him as a teacher. He taught me well enough that I passed into high school with honours.

"One of our popular activities was cadets. It was taken very seriously. We had just passed through the first world war. Our instructors, Lieutenant Russell Copeland and Lieutenant Day Warnica had both just returned from the war. An honourary fixture was General John Hughes, the brother of Sir Sam Hughes, Canada's Minister of War. General Hughes lived on Wellington Street just across from the school and west a bit. There was always a Union Jack flying from his flag pole. He always addressed the cadets on inspection day. His uniform was most impressive.

"For school lighting, I don't remember either coal oil lamps or candles. On dull days the teacher used yellow chalk on the blackboard as it showed up better than white. I believe the school was wired for electricity about 1921 or 22 as I had been at school for four or five years. For heat we had two large hot air furnaces and soft coal was used. Each room had a large register and the teacher controlled the heat by opening and closing a large vent to the register.

"I only remember seeing a nurse once during my time at Central. She measured our height, and checked our eyes, ears, nose and throat and our teeth. She also checked our hair for lice as they went through the school once while I was there. We were given a report to take home of her findings.

"Around 1917 we had a smallpox epidemic. Every pupil had to be vaccinated in order to attend school. I had a note from the doctor allowing me to attend school without being vaccinated as my heart was too weak after being sick for nearly a whole year. I still have not been vaccinated. Most pupils had a terrible reaction to the vaccine. Some had sore and swollen arms and were real ill for a few days. Pupils with sore arms wore a red cloth sewn on their coat. They were the majority and at recess looking out over the schoolyard it was just a sea of red arm bands.

"The school concert was put on each year in the auditorium of the town hall. It was mostly choral singing, quartets and some short skits. It was always under Miss Helen Morris. It was all part of her job as a teacher. I never heard of her being paid extra. On the last of the three nights she was always given flowers.

"I don't think we had a school concert the year the flu epidemic hit. Crowds were discouraged. The flu was blamed on the returning soldiers from Europe.

"There were special days. On Valentine's Day we had a post office for our class only. I always felt sorry for a few girls and boys who received only one or two cards. At Christmas we had a small class party with recitations of poetry and class singing of Christmas carols. It was a big deal to eat cookies and candies at our desk. I don't remember having pop, just water out of the fountain.

"We started school using a slate and slate pencil. Near the end of the first year we were allowed to use lead pencils. I believe I was at school at least three years before we were allowed to use pen and ink. Fountain pens were off in the future. We had pen nibs fitted into a holder and dipped the pen into an ink well counter sunk in our desk.

"We had mostly double seats. The greatest punishment for misbehaving was to be told to sit in a double seat beside a girl."[2]

Stu loved sports and played for Bowmanville's High School's first football team in 1928, and in that same year was a member of the Bowmanville Owls hockey team which almost won a junior championship.[3] He had many friends. One was Al Osborne, a gifted athlete who once pitched the local team to victory over a touring black all-star team in the 1940s; hosted a touring East Asian badminton team after it had been barred from Toronto's Granite Club; and later operated Bowmanville's bowling alley. Bill Bagnell was a brilliant runner and teacher at the local boys' training school and was the special guest at the Bowmanville Museum's annual 10 kilometre run in 1995. Bob Kent was another. From his Lowe Street home he recalled his grandfather's electrical demonstrations at local schools. His proudest accomplishment was over fifty years of service at the Lions Club on Beech Avenue. These were all men who loved to sit on verandas or in coffee shops and tell wonderful stories of Bowmanville's small town life in the 20th century.

Stu might have drifted from job to job, but after driving a truck for two years for the Vanstone Mill he was offered a position inside in 1936. When the old miller, William Cole, fell ill, Stu took over and began an almost forty year career which ended only after a bad fall at the dam. The mill is unquestionably

Stuart Candler, last of the millers at the Vanstone Mill, stands by a hopper in the mill, July 21, 1982. On this day, official opening ceremonies were held by new owner, Ralph Pypker.

the most significant historic structure and site in Bowmanville. It was built in the late 1840s under a partnership of John Simpson and John Burk (on the site of an even earlier mill built by Burk). It was known as the "Big Mill" and was later owned by Charles Bowman's heir, Elizabeth Raynes. It was in turn sold to the Vanstone family in 1886.

The wheat producing region of Canada moved west in the late 19th century. Milling businesses in the east declined, but the Vanstone Mill survived by importing huge quantities of wheat. The Second World War gave it new life and importance. Vanstone's returned to the export business and continued after the war sending their products to Egypt, Ceylon, Israel, and the British Isles. In the sixties the Russians made large purchases of Canadian flour and much of Vanstone's product was shipped to Cuba.[4]

Stu's accident and the aging of the equipment occurred almost simultaneously. He retired and the mill was stripped of its equipment. The local conservation authority had already expended its limited funds buying a mill north of Bowmanville so the contents of the Vanstone Mill were sold out of the community. The Vanstone family sold the mill building and it reverted to a shell retailing a variety of product.

Before his death Stu told thousands of stories and kept to himself many others that were perhaps the "real" story of Bowmanville's everyday life. There is much that cannot be told except in fiction, but one tale suffices. "Mr. Tilley's mother employed a housemaid who had three children out of wedlock. The wife of the Anglican minister, Major Spencer, wrote to Tilley sometime in the 1930s, telling him that such a woman was of poor character for such a job. Tilley responded that he was unaware she had three children and would immediately raise her pay. She got a good recommendation after Mrs. Tilley's death and moved to Hamilton."[5]

Finally there is one personal memory of Stu. Shortly after my arrival in Bowmanville in 1974, my grandparents suggested there may have been a link between our family history and Bowmanville. This seemed absurd. My wife and I, who had both grown up at Yonge and Eglinton in Toronto, had only come to Bowmanville in 1974 because she found her first teaching job here.

In 1976 I visited Stu to learn more about the mills of Bowmanville and in the course of that conversation showed him a picture of my great grandmother Elizabeth Candler. Stu proclaimed, "That's Aunt Liz." She was one of the thirteen children of John Candler and Ann Rhem, and she left Bowmanville with her parents in the 1880s.

Sometime in the 1920s she and her young son Arthur (Westlake), my grandfather, had visited her former home in Bowmanville. In the course of that visit Arthur and Stu had stolen a boat at Port Darlington and gone for a proverbial "joy ride" on Lake Ontario.

In 1977 Stu and his wife Bea and my grandparents met for the only time at our home on Beech Avenue. There Stu and my grandfather reminisced about those days long ago in Bowmanville. Curiously a police car drove up and down our street all night and we speculated they were just keeping watch to make sure no boats were stolen.

Those folks on our verandah are all gone now, but their connection to Bowmanville's life is part of the town's story.

Notes

[1] From interviews with Arthur Westlake and Stu Candler in the 1970s and 80s.

[2] Ibid

[3] "Stu Candler played centre and in those days fell back to defence when the defence rushed up the ice…The game was played before the era of the forward pass and each man had to be an individualist, able to stick-handle, give and receive a pass on side." As written by "The Kingfish" in *The Canadian Statesman*, 10 July 1955.

[4] From notes provided by Stu Candler and sources including Squair, and Hamlyn, Lunney and Morrison.

[5] From interviews with Stu Candler.

Chapter Eleven

He Has Done Some Good in the Community

"Every landscape of any size or age has a style of its own, a period style such as we discern or try to discern in music or architecture or painting, and a landscape true to its style, containing enough of the diagnostic traits, whether if it is in Appalachia or Southern California, can give an almost aesthetic satisfaction. By accepting this admittedly superficial approach, we can I think, learn to define other unknown landscapes, provided we know the necessary traits."

– J.B. Jackson, *Discovering the Vernacular Landscape*

"You know, we get a bit fed up now and then with those who run down Bowmanville as a small, jerk-water hamlet, with lousy organizations, no entertainment, frowzy-looking stores and all the rest. These perpetual bigtimers who wouldn't go to anything here if it was free with a lunch thrown in, and wouldn't buy anything locally if they could obtain it in Oshawa or Toronto, make us sick."[1]

So editorialized *The Canadian Statesman*, under the headline "Who Says This Is a Small Town?" What followed was a somewhat nervous protestation in its 13 December 1961 edition which betrayed the community's desire to be, if not bigger in size, then certainly more respected in the estimation of outsiders. Too often this feeling has degenerated in many towns into a purposeless pursuit of both a larger population and any development, regardless of its contribution to the town's long term viability or the enhancement of its historic character and continuance of tradition.

The editorial followed the staging of Bowmanville's first Santa Claus Parade which has since become an annual rite of the Christmas season. The arrival of Santa Claus by parade replicates mythological stories of the stranger or outsider arriving in town. Such newcomers are usually greeted with suspicion and hostility, so the Santa visitor bringing gifts has a gentle purpose in North America. The irony cannot be lost in the case of Bowmanville where a half century of slow change was being replaced by external forces.

The Santa Claus Parade, despite *The Statesman's* headline, celebrated small town virtue in its cast of participants. According to *The Statesman*, they included Mayor Wilfred Carruthers in Councillor Wesley Fice's gaily decorated

78

sound truck, the pretty Bowmanville Bluettes directed by Irenie Harvey, the traditional music of the local Salvation Army Band, four smart ponies driven by Ray Cochrane of Enniskillen, Joy-Anne's "eye-catching" Peterborough Majorettes, the hilarious antics of the famed Belleville Clown Band, the stimulating music played by the Ontario Training School for Boys' Band commanded by Lieutenant W.W. Bagnell and the prize-winning Bowmanville Legion Pipe Band. The joyous climax of the parade was the appearance of Santa Claus, played, said *The Statesman*, to absolute perfection by Dr. H.B. Rundle.

The parade became a marvellous demonstration of how small communities can retain their character in the midst of creating new traditions. More significantly it was the first great continuous public celebration in Bowmanville's 20th century evolution. The 1958 Centennial event had been a one-time occurrence with no lasting impact on local self perception.

The relative stagnation in the community's physical and cultural development following the economic upheaval in Bowmanville's industrial life at the turn of the century, hides a vibrant local lifestyle of which snatches can be glimpsed through the local paper and the memory of the town's elder citizens. Some of these were reported in the same edition in which the parade story appeared. It noted that Baron Von Mullenhein, a survivor of the sinking of the German battleship, the *Bismarck*, had recently visited his former residence at the Bowmanville Training School which had served as a Prisoner of War Camp.

It was also reported that Alfie Shrubb had celebrated his 82nd birthday at his daughter's house on Prince Street. Shrubb had operated the Cream of Barley Mill for many years in Bowmanville, but was better known as perhaps the world's premier long distance runner in the first decade of the 20th century when, running for his native Britain, he held many world records and ran a series of famous match races against the Canadian Native runner, Tom Longboat. George James of *The Statesman* was instrumental in bringing Shrubb to Bowmanville in the 1930s, a testament as much as anything to James' powers of persuasion and his own reputation and friendships which far exceeded the boundaries of most small town journalists.

One can proceed only randomly through these stories looking less for any meaningful connections between them than for the elements of small town life in which everyday common experiences are recorded for posterity in the local paper. These would have been ignored, unknown or forgotten by their participants in a larger town. There are, as well, stories surprising in their vigour, tragedy and scandal, which are not so easily ignored yet are swept quickly under the carpet of small town remembrance. In many cases these stories include people one sees tomorrow on the street or they damage an already insecure local pride.

From a typical week in early September 1912, *The Statesman* reported that Mr. and Mrs. Solomon Cartwright Hillier were on a trip to Cleveland and

Akron, Ohio, Mr. Frank Kydd was back from Cuba, Lieutenant Morris had won nearly all the best prizes at the Ontario Rifle Association meet in Toronto, Miss Regina Percy on Silver Street will resume her class in piano and Mr. T.E. Higginbotham received a beautiful wreath from the Victoria Hockey Club of Winnipeg on Labour Day, this being the anniversary of the death of his brother, Mr. Fred T. Higginbotham who was accidentally killed in that city. "This is the 16th time this club has sent a floral offering to be placed on their comrade's grave. At the annual meeting in October at the roll call of the membership the acknowledgment is always read in response to his name."[2]

Higginbotham had gone west in the 1880s and was a star lacrosse player. With skating skills learned on the frozen ponds of Bowmanville he played hockey in the winter and was a member of the Winnipeg team which won the Stanley Cup in early 1896. Then, in the late summer, he fell from a horse at a teammate's home, broke his spinal cord and died in agony within twelve hours. Higginbotham's body was shipped home to Bowmanville. He was buried in the local cemetery beside an impressive monument on which rests a huge orb donated by his teammates and still visible from the road today. His shocked hockey colleagues lost the Cup that December to the visiting Montreal team.[3]

As well, in 1912, an electric line of the Toronto and Eastern Railway reached Bowmanville.[4] Plans envisioned railcars crossing Vanstone's Pond on a wooden bridge, passing over Scugog Street and moving along Wellington Street as far as Liberty where they would reverse for the return to Toronto. The line never operated and though Ontario Hydro had an interest in taking it over,

Tait's Camp on Bowmanville's beach in the summer of 1893.

Bowmanville's own short wave radio station.

the automobile had condemned it to an aborted delivery. The Railway was a last hurrah for the 19th century dream of train travel. In its planned use of large storage batteries, however, it may also have been a precursor of transportation technology in the 21st century. Unfortunately it had no place in the century in which it was built.

In the 1920s Bowmanville entered the media age with its own small radio station operated by Christian Rehder, owner of the Bowmanville Foundry. "He always had to have the first of everything," his son, Tom, says, "but at its peak the radio signal was picked up as far away as Cuba."

Rehder's small town station featured Methodist and Presbyterian church services, as well as local performers like Scott's Orchestra (Lewis Scott, Clarence Bombard and Miss Heloise Thickson), Wilbert Oke on Hawaiian guitar, Fred Tuerk on piccolo, pianist Gwendolyn Williams and vocalists Ruby and Irene Hallman. Bowmanville High School's public speaking winners were broadcast, Dr. Hazlewood lectured on "How to Avoid the Flu" and Dr. Bonnycastle and Major Gill gave short speeches on Armistice Day.[5]

In the late summer of 1936 *The Statesman* reported the construction of a new reception and hospital building at the Boys' Training School on Concession Street, a site later included in Paul Quarrington's book *King Leary*. The local Bowmanville Royals baseball club won the Lakeshore League title for the third season beating Picton in three straight games. Miss Alice Medd had accepted a position with the Zellers store in Oshawa. Mrs. E.C.C. Southey's son Jimmy who had been holidaying in the Limestone City (Kingston) returned home with her.[6]

Perhaps most significantly in April of that year the principal of the town's major primary school, Central Public, was dismissed after it was alleged that copying had been condoned during final exams.[7] Parents responded by charging that his replacement was a man known for his rather severe enforcement of corporal punishment. A petition in support of the principal's re-instatement was delivered to the Board, but they proceeded with the action. Shortly after Easter, Andy Thompson arrived from Toronto to assume the post.

Students staged an impromptu walk-out and *The Toronto Globe* editorialized that "...the strike is a manifestation of the respect at least one teacher of the Bowmanville school can command from the students."[8] Even the provincial Minister of Education, Dr. L.J. Simpson, got involved suggesting that the end of the strike "...would serve to bring about a quicker settlement."[9]

Andy Thompson recalls that while students gradually straggled back to class matters did not return to normal until the next school year. The former principal remained on staff as agriculture teacher until his retirement in 1940. Thompson was at the school until 1949 and became the senior and respected administrator of local Bowmanville public schools thereafter, while assuming a host of community roles in his adopted hometown.

One of the most tragic local consequences of the Second World War, in which Canadians fought from 1939 through 1945, was the deaths of three Bowmanville brothers, Bill, Alec and Sandy Colville while serving as pilots between 1942 and 1944. *The Toronto Star* reported in 1946, "The boys' father died in 1942, after the death of their first son. The only member of the once happy family that Mrs. Colville has at home now is her daughter Katherine." In 1996 a Memorial Clock Tower was dedicated in the brothers' memory at the newly designed Rotary Park at the southern end of Temperance Street where the town's arena had operated from 1949 to 1988.[10]

One of the war's legacies was the continuation of the cadet program at the Bowmanville High School until well into the 1950s. Under Principal Louis Dippell, the entire school body put down their books in May and donned uniforms, drilled and occasionally fired rifles in order that the school might collect an annual stipend on inspection by the regimental brass from Kingston.

Occasionally *The Statesman* reported bizarre tales suggesting both a more fanciful yet darker world unique to the combination of town and country in near proximity. Such was the tale of the "Ghost of the Kingston Road" reported on 19 April 1945 in which the figure of a man in white making the motions of swinging a scythe or cradle was recalled from around 1880. A harvest moon, the witching hour of midnight, an orchard and the tiny community of Maple Grove, just west of Bowmanville, were the ingredients of the first sighting. By the time locals had gathered it became apparent the ghost was simply a farmer clad only in a nightshirt.[11] But almost sixty-five years later the myth of the ghost and the mystery of the tale retained its power and memory.

In that same decade the last vestiges of temperance were flourishing. A *Statesman* advertisement of 12 February 1948 noted that Bowmanville had a hotel "...without either Beer Room profits or special subsidies". Thus it was that citizens of nearby Newcastle, five miles east, were asked to vote against proposed "women's beer rooms" or as the resolution noted, "Are you in favour of the continuance of the sale of beer only under Public House License for consumption on licensed premises to which women are admitted?"[12]

On the other hand organizations like the Four Freedoms League and the Newcastle Citizens League said that a "...a majority of them are public spirited law-abiding citizens, and will acquire their beverages by other legal channels when the Women's Beer Rooms are closed."[13] The alternative some suggested was either legal sale or sale through the bootlegger. If women were deprived of access to a beverage room "...how will they vote when the question comes up for the continuance of the men's beverage room?"[14]

In 1958 Bowmanville celebrated its centennial and perhaps the finest moment was the carrying of a ceremonial torch by Alfie Shrubb. A half century of stagnation, however, was now becoming apparent in what had been some of Bowmanville's prized features. The lakefront once featured the busy port of Darlington from which grain was shipped to Oswego throughout much of the 19th century. The McKinley Tariff ended such trade, but it was replaced by pleasure cruises to Toronto or around the harbour, often featuring David Morrison Senior's Orchestra.[15] The train then brought the middle class of Toronto to the cottage community which grew by the lake in the first half of the 20th century. By the 1950s, however, those cottagers had cars and they travelled further afield to the Kawarthas or Muskoka. The cottage area intended only for summer use was gradually taken over by families looking for year round affordable housing. Not surprisingly the area declined in appearance and reputation.

In early June 1962, in the same week that Canada's Prime Minister John Diefenbaker visited Bowmanville, a huge siren was installed atop the town hall as "...a precaution should there ever be a nuclear war." It was the clearest demonstration that war, which until then had been a distant phenomenon involving South Africa at the turn of the century and the deaths of many young Bowmanville men on two occasions in Europe, was suddenly in the town's backyard.

Meanwhile Diefenbaker[16] reinforced the locals sense of self with his comment on "your beautiful countryside," a recurring theme which touched on the defining character of Bowmanville and its surroundings.

In May 1964 the Boston Bruins thanked Bowmanville for the use of the town's arena by their junior club, the Oshawa Generals, while a new arena was built in Oshawa. As a result local citizens regularly saw a future National Hockey League great, Bobby Orr.[17]

Bowmanville Harbour.

The increasing invasion of the outside world as benignly symbolized by the Santa Claus Parade was dramatically and more ambivalently demonstrated by four separate incidents in the last part of the 1960s.

Few issues more clearly defined the changing feature of small town life than those involving either alcohol and religion. It might be said that the latter occupied a declining influence on the mainstream character of life throughout the 20th century, but that loss was felt more deeply in communities with roots and a stronger sense of public solidarity.

Symbolizing this issue was the vote on Sunday sports and movies held in April 1962 in response to changes in Ontario's Lord's Day Act of 1960.[18] On the yes side stood sportsman like *Statesman* columnist, Frank Mohun, who said, "...because I play golf and Goodyear hockey on Sundays throughout the year, it wouldn't be fair if I voted against Sunday sports—so the baseball players, bowlers, etc. would be unable to play, while I continued my sporting activities." For Mohun it was a matter of equity.

On the other hand the Bowmanville Ministerial Association called the proposal a desecration of the Sabbath and an attack on both the family and a stable community life. "When the Sunday is used for secular purposes, the moral foundation of society will be undermined," they said. The ministers correctly noted the trend towards a more open Sunday and decried its impact. "If we whittle away at the sanctity of the Lord's Day, we are whittling away at the moral foundations of society and the nation."[19]

The Statesman acknowledged its Methodist background, but found something hypocritical in opposing sports and movies in one's own town while

Alfred Shrubb, left, manager, and James Lake Morden, owner of Bowmanville's Cream of Barley Mill, camp and park, 1928.

attending shows or a hockey game in Toronto. "Why should similar places in Bowmanville not be allowed to operate? Are we so much purer at home or are we to be numbered among the hypocrites who feel that everything we do is right, provided our neighbours don't see us?"[20]

The ministers' appeal had lost its ability to inflame passions like it might have done in an earlier era. It's likely that Bowmanville's still significant church going populace probably supported an open Sunday though a private ballot prevented full disclosure. For Sunday sports the vote was 696 "yes" against 451 "no", while Sunday movies gained support from 637 against 457 not in favour.

A second sign was the Drama Workshop presentation in March 1965 of "The Waltz of the Toreadors" which *The Statesman* deemed as "adult entertainment" and which "showed lack of discretion."[21] While commending the performers, *The Statesman* thundered, "Surely we have not reached the stage here in our development, sophistication or morality when infidelity, seduction, obvious lust and a continuous stream of blasphemy accompanied by all too obvious intimacies are welcomed and applauded as normal from a local stage…we found it hard to concentrate on the performance and instead couldn't help wondering about the reactions of the mother and daughter who sat directly in front of us."[22] It was the clash of two cultures, one a perhaps better educated newer resident against an older more socially conservative long-time resident.

A year later the town was stunned with the discovery of the theft from municipal funds of over $38,000 by Bowmanville's clerk between 1961 and

1965. He was given a suspended sentence which drew protest from the Crown Attorney, but disbelief in a small town where honesty and leaving doors unlocked was an article of faith.[23]

Finally in 1970 a huge rock festival dubbed Strawberry Fields was held at the Mosport Race Track, about eight miles north of Bowmanville.[24] According to Stu Candler, in the days before and after the concert many attendees from all parts of Canada and the United States went skinnydipping in the Vanstone's Pond in imitation of the Woodstock festival the year before. In microcosm these events suggested a changing world, drawing Bowmanville gradually out of the more insular life of the first half of the 20th century.

In 1962 one of the great people of Bowmanville life in the first half of the century, George James, *The Statesman* editor, died—"...not only Bowmanville but Canada has lost a distinguished and talented citizen."[25]

Band of the Ontario Training School for Boys, Bowmanville, parading on King Street near the intersection of Temperance Street, circa 1955–60. To the right of photo are former Bank of Montreal building and former post office building, now both demolished.

He had operated *The Statesman* for fifty years until selling his interest to his nephew John in 1958. At one time or another he was mayor of Bowmanville, a town councillor, treasurer of Trinity United Church, one of the major fund raisers for construction of Bowmanville Memorial Hospital, a good soccer goal-keeper and a man who liked to argue politics and baseball. He was recipient of an honourary doctor of law degree from Queen's University. Under him the paper supported the Conservatives, but his nephew John ran and won in 1949 as a Liberal candidate in Durham riding.

He retained a deep understanding of the nature of small town life and its press. "A paper is a semi-public institution. You should leave it and the community better than you found them," he said.[26] And of the country editor, he noted, "Even your enemies are good enemies, and a good enemy is almost as good as a good friend."[27]

"I can't think," James said, "of a better epitaph than this: Here lies George James. He has done some good in the community."[28]

Notes

[1] *The Canadian Statesman*, 13 December 1961.

[2] *The Canadian Statesman*, 5 September 1912.

[3] *The Winnipeg Daily Tribune*, 8 September 1896; *The Canadian Statesman*, 16 September 1896; *The Canadian Statesman*, 28 February 1900.

[4] Clayton Morgan, "Bommanville's Mysterious Electric Railway," *Bowmanville Downtowner*. Vol. 1 Issue 3, November 1994.

[5] Newsletter of Bowmanville Radio Club, Operating 10 A.E., as reproduced from *The Canadian Statesman* (undated).

[6] *The Canadian Statesman*, 3 September 1936.

[7] Falls, Hobson, and Humber, "A Centennial Celebration," *Central Public School 1889-1989*, pp. 32-34.

[8] *The Toronto Globe*, 10 April 1936.

[9] *The Canadian Statesman*, 23 April 1936.

[10] *The Belvedere (Quarterly Journal of the Bowmanville Museum) No. 3* 1992; Program of the Official Opening of Rotary Park and Dedication of Colville Memorial Clock Tower, 2 June 1996.

[11] From a letter by H.G. Hutcheson of Port Perry appearing in *The Canadian Statesman*, 19 April 1945.

[12] *The Canadian Statesman*, 12 February 1948.

[13] Ibid

[14] "Hotels, NOT Beer Rooms, are beneficial to the community. So vote out Women's Beer Rooms on February 18th...", from *The Canadian Statesman*, 12 February 1948.

[15] Hamlyn, Lunney, and Morrison, Bowmanville: A Retrospect, p. 48b.

[16] *The Canadian Statesman*, 6 June 1962.

[17] *The Canadian Statesman*, 13 May 1964.

[18] *The Canadian Statesman*, 4 April 1962, and 11 April 1962.

[19] Ibid

[20] Ibid

[21] *The Canadian Statesman*, 10 March 1965. A Statesman editorial described the play as "… a comedy that was as "out-of-line", as anything we have seen here." For weeks after debates raged in the Statesman between those for and against the newspaper's point of view.

[22] Ibid

[23] *The Canadian Statesman*, 16 March 1966.

[24] *Toronto Globe and Mail*, 8 August 1970.

[25] *The Canadian Statesman*, 2 May 1962, and 9 May 1962.

[26] Ibid

[27] Ibid

[28] Ibid

Chapter Twelve

Town Landmark Gives Way to Community Progress

"You all know how the atmosphere of an old house is quite different from that of a newly built one. There is some other quality about it which touches you as soon as you walk through the door. And what is that, but the spirit of the place. It's not just some ghost hovering over the roof, but part of the bricks, part of the furniture, part of the floor, part of the walls. That is what I mean when I tell you that the spirits are among us, and are a part of us."

– Peter Ackroyd, *English Music*

While we have come to associate major urban change in Bowmanville with developments beginning in the late 1980s, a vision of the future was afforded throughout the 1960s. Bowmanville and other small towns began to come out of their half century stagnation and the usual response in looking at the growth and allure of nearby Toronto was to destroy as much of its own past as possible and replace it with a particularly stale idea of a "modern" society.

The unchanging face of main street became a kind of effrontery to the notion of progress. Ideas of creative revitalization and renaissance communities which are common today were more likely to be overshadowed in the sixties by the brutal force of urban renewal. The fate of main street is in many ways a microcosm of that of the entire small town. Its desecration through competition from mall and strip development on the urban fringe is a sword touched with two sides. Protection of downtown against competition inevitably means higher costs which in turn send consumers farther afield to nearby towns for bargains. On the other hand restriction of competition allows for a certain downtown prosperity and maintenance of urban character.

In early 1962 Dr. Breslin, a landowner in the area, blasted the people of Bowmanville for the lack of industrial expansion and the generally backward character of the town. This blow to local pride was dealt with by the defensive suggestion that only those who spend money in the town should criticize it. Such behaviour would be acceptable, for instance, for Dr. Breslin's brother who had for years operated a successful women's wear shop in town.[1]

Still there was an awareness that Bowmanville had a problem. As early as 1953 *The Statesman* wondered, "Is it time for change in local store hours?"[2]

Digging is in progress prior to the laying of the pipes for the first waterworks in Bowmanville, 1912–13. The location is near the north side of King Street just east of Division. The Balmoral Hotel (Castle today) is the building on the upper right of this picture.

In those days banks closed on Saturdays and retail outlets on Wednesday forcing the surrounding countryside to do its business on Thursday and Friday.

Main Street businesses over the years ranged from the oddly eclectic such as the short lived Palm Readers and Counsellors who came and went in early 1961,[3] to the venerable Stedman's which arrived in 1963 and lasted thirty years.[4] It advertised coffee tables, tape recorders, stereo hi-fi sets, exquisite crystal, a pet department, lawn mowers, marvellous brass ware from India, hit parade long play records and an excellent shoe department. By its demise virtually all these features had long since departed to the more extensive retail outlets in Oshawa.

Main street Bowmanville of 1961 was the topic of a *Statesman* editorial which took umbrage with those who suggested the town hadn't changed in thirty-five years. In place of Couch, Johnston and Cryderman's store was Lloyd Ellis Shoe Store. The Royal Theatre was playing Hoot Gibson in the mid twenties whereas a Ben Hur festival would be featured in the early sixties. Elsewhere in 1926, "G.Alex Edmonstone was selling meat. Leo G. Greenaway advertised Hecla furnaces. C.M. Cawker and Son were butchers in the Victoria Building and Lance Phare and Garnet McCoy had just opened a new butcher shop in the Cowan Block. Tom Dustan's Hardware, now Maher's, was holding a Dollar Day. S.W. Mason and Son was celebrating its 50th anniversary in Dry Goods. Mason and Dale Hardware had stove pipes at 20 cents a length and Harry Allin (now McQuinn's) advertised olives. R.M. Mitchell and Co. (McGregor's Drugs) was promoting improved eyesight and Edith V. Scobell (Abernethy's) sold insurance."[5]

In 1996, thirty-five years after that *Statesman* story, the stores on main street were places like Rickaby's, once W. Allen's Big 20 Bookstore. Colonel Sam McLaughlin was perhaps Rickaby's most famous patron. Gary Cole cut hair in the same Spanish-flavoured building where his grandfather Jack located in the early years of the depression. The building had been erected by wealthy druggist, J.H. Jury on the former site of a Chinese laundry and a store selling flour and eggs.[6] According to one source Jury's advertised a cancer cure medicine for $15. It was made in the Organ factory and people sent money from all over the United States and Canada. The workers used to drink the tonic and said they liked it. In defense it was claimed that it didn't kill anyone. (Didn't help anyone either.)

Typical of the confused attitude to the town's past were reports on the loss of old buildings. "Town Landmark Gives Way to Community Progress" headlined *The Statesman* on 13 December, 1961 announcing the tearing down of several buildings housing Sutton's Barber Shop, George Somerscales's TV Shop, Goheen's Handy Store and the Astor Photo Studio. A "modern, new supermarket" was planned for the site. The unquenchable faith in the modern and progress was part of the ideology of change which embraced newness as a reflection of an active business community. More darkly, however, it was also a statement of despair about the lost ambition of the small town and the need to eradicate the past if it was to go forward.

Is historic preservation a useful idea for a community? It would seem the historian has need to embrace it. But for what reason? It is certainly a key memory of the past with its lessons. For the present it provides temporal connectivity, and security. For the future it preserves a piece of the built environment which has often as not served to define a larger streetscape and even townscape within explicit boundaries. It provides, as well, direction for future development to follow seen models.

On the other hand there are pieces of the past such as the water tower at the CPR station torn down in May 1961 and marked in the paper by the headline "Old Landmark Being Torn Down"[7] which attracted attention only because "the inside wood was almost as good as the day it was put up." It was a reminder of a time before the "dieselation of the railway engines." Its preservation lies on shakier grounds perhaps because items of an industrial period have less power to evoke identification.

The 8 June 1966 *The Statesman* included a more reflective headline. "Take a Final Look at Old Post Office," as the old Post Office, built in 1903 at the corner of Temperance and King and later converted to the library, was torn down by its owner, the Bank of Montreal. "The familiar town clock probably will be missed more than any other part of the structure," *The Statesman* said.[8] The building hugged the corner of the street and provided a lovely definition for the sidewalk and street. Its four story prominence corresponded to much of the rest of King and its grandeur suggested perhaps more about the town's ambition than its history realized. Its replacement by a one story structure with no architectural interest not only deprived the street of some of its visual charm, but it reduced the overall impact of Bowmanville's main four corners with the loss of one of their defining features.

It was almost as devastating a historic blow as the loss in the same period of the original Ontario Bank building immediately to the west. It had carried "dignity and permanence" in its facade. Together with the Horsey Block in its original brick on the northeast corner, the view along the north of King Street had been that of a small town which may have lost much of its industry at the turn of the century, but still communicated its role as a significant centre in at least the Northumberland and Durham area. The Horsey Block was the last to go and the view now is decidedly common, shallow and quotidian.

As late as 11 August 1976 *The Statesman* photographed Oshawa developer Mario Veltri directing Mayor Garnet Rickard in the demolition of the old bus

Beech Avenue (incorrectly spelled as Beach). William C. King's house is shown in foreground with his daughter's income property and home next door.

station and badminton hall. "Demolition on Two Local Landmarks Underway," *The Statesman* said and continued, "The new building will be a big step forward in replacing two structures along King Street that have historic significance but in recent years have become eyesores."[9] This begs the question of why they had become eyesores, but in their place arose Bowmanville's first significant high-rise, a building without any redeeming architectural, and only limited streetscape merit. It was a reminder of an old joke about the real estate agent trying to convince a couple to buy the penthouse in a large building of a quaint New England town because "The view is great and you can't see the only eyesore in town because you live in it."

The issue of loss was one that continues into the present. There was perhaps no sadder historic loss however than the old Dominion Organ and Piano Building in 1990 which, because of its length, height, and contribution to the streetscape of Temperance, was a remarkable survivor of an older industrial period. Architect Jack Diamond had actually shown plans for its incorporation in the plans for the old Town Hall which was itself renovated in the mid eighties. It was not to be, nor were initial development designs envisioning its creative reuse for retail and residential purposes. By the end of the decade the town council of Newcastle (now Clarington) rather lamely acquiesced to a developer's request for a demolition permit. The loss was historically tragic particularly since, as Diamond and others envisioned, its reuse for town administrative purposes was not beyond the impossible only the imaginable.

As significant for the town's future in the 1960s were developments which suggested a new, distinctly anti-urban trend. In the early sixties the nearby town of Port Hope expressed alarm at the impact of service centres on Highway 401 and the loss of $300,000 worth of annual main street business. The opening of the 401 in Scarborough in 1956, linking Eastern Ontario with Toronto, permanently changed the orientation of communities. For Bowmanville this meant the end of a century old focus on Port Hope and Cobourg though this would only be confirmed with the introduction of regional government in 1974. It was now easier for people in Bowmanville to commute for work, pleasure or shopping in the big city to the west.

It was also reported that Bowmanville's first shopping centre would be built off Highway 2 in the eastern end of the town though it was a small strip retail structure with little impact on the older downtown.[10] In 1962 *The Statesman* advertised new homes in the Parkway Crescent Sub-Division one of the first significant housing developments in town since the 19th century.[11] The slight growth in town population made letter carrier delivery possible. Prior to 1966 citizens paid daily visits to the post office to pick up their mail.

A feature of Bowmanville life hardly visible to either new residents or those passing quickly through town was the social dividing line roughly at Highway 2 or King Street between the north and south wards of town.[12] The south, particularly

Staff of the Goodyear Tire and Rubber Company, Bowmanville, circa 1910–15.

that area below Queen Street, was working class focused around the Goodyear Factory. The north, particularly that area below the CPR tracks, included the managers, and professionals of Bowmanville who lived in the town's larger homes (of the area north of the CPR tracks Mary Jewell says it was somewhat sarcastically known as English Town perhaps because its social pretensions did not always match its economic strength). Stories are told of young women raised in the south ward who, on marrying north ward boys, spent their entire lives contemplating their unworthiness to live there.

The sidewalks of Bowmanville reflect this history. Several generations of politicians including the "Goodyear Council", so named because for a period all members of the town council were affiliated with Goodyear, rejected cement and approved the tarmacking of town sidewalks. They argued that the widows of Goodyear workers could not support town taxes based on "extravagant" public works. One of those Goodyear "politicos" was Ken Hooper who, in his schooldays had been a leader of the infamous strike at Central School in 1936, an experience that shaped his later union and town council participation.

In the north ward locals had the power to counteract questionable political decisions. Council had decided in 1966 that Beech Ave. would be a one-way street with parking forbidden.[13] Road widening was also discussed. All three features of this discussion reflected a planning bias that in many cases still prevails.

Any one of these actions would have been disastrous for the street and its ambience. The plans were not realized and the street today remains narrow, parking is allowed and cars flow both ways. It may lead to small traffic tie-ups as people attempt to reach the Lions Centre on the west side of the street, but it also slows cars, allows people to walk in relative safety and permits the street to function as a proper neighbourhood for the majority of time when few cars use it. It was apparent, nevertheless, that the old character and image of the town was undergoing alterations of an unpredictable sort.

Formal planning in the town had been somewhat of an academic exercise during a period of little growth, but now Bowmanville was starting to attract attention. In March 1962, twenty-three students in the Division of Town and Regional Planning, School of Architecture of the University of Toronto presented their study of the town's future at council chambers.[14] For all of its recommendations *The Statesman* focused on a potential population of 18,000 by 1981 a figure not realized due to inadequate water and sewer services. The report suggested a central mall or civic square in the town, critiqued the present strip development along King Street and suggested the widening of many streets. The notion of a square of sorts was finally realized in the 1996 Rotary Park. Bowmanville then, was as it would remain until the mid 1990s, largely focused around its downtown and its commercial growth was along Highway 2. This allowed the town to retain its small town character though often the lack of retail variety sent residents to Oshawa or even Toronto.

With growth, the report's authors said, "It will lose its character as the centre of an agricultural district, and become a thriving small industrial and

A 1946 view of the south side of King Street, just west of Temperance. Seen prominently is the front of D.A. McGregor's pharmacy at 5 King Street West. The sign over the doorway was installed in September of 1936.

commercial centre."[15] The report accepts the inevitability of a certain kind of progress and growth. It paid little attention to either the nature or historic character of the town and the possibility of using these features as a basis for planning the town's future. It even proposed the demolition of Central Public School, a neighbourhood facility that still functions remarkably well thirty-five years later.

This lack of vision continues to bedevil many small towns. Nevertheless an editorial of that day saluted the students' work. "Optimism grips the Community," said *The Statesman* in 1962.[16] Local gloom and pessimism had been replaced by forecasts of "…considerable growth and expansion for this entire area." This, of course, was a prediction which embittered "…the negative thinkers who see Bowmanville as a small town forever."

Ironically an editorial in the same issue of the *Statesman* also suggested that "…some folks just can't seem to understand our way of life in a comparatively small community. The fact that almost everyone knows your business, your hours of rising and retiring, your every move, is too much for those who have been accustomed to city life, where quite frequently you have no idea who lives next door… and care less."[17] The story in question described a neighbouring paper's misrepresentation of a local individual about whom the word prosecution should have appeared and not, as in fact happened, the word, "prostitution." Despite these potential calamities of a small town it is clear the editor would have no other life. Yet while the paper celebrated this way of life, it also favourably described developments and growth that would make Bowmanville a kind of half way place with few of the endearing features of a small town and none of the benefits of a much larger urban centre.

Notes

[1] *The Canadian Statesman*, 31 January 1962.
[2] *The Canadian Statesman*, 29 October 1953.
[3] *The Canadian Statesman*, 29 March 1961.
[4] *The Canadian Statesman*, 8 May 1963.
[5] *The Canadian Statesman*, 19 April 1961.
[6] *The Oshawa Times EXTRA*, 27 February 1961.
[7] *The Canadian Statesman*, 24 May 1961. "Way back in 1913, the construction of this water tower at the CPR station must have been a big event, because it marked the introduction of a second railway to this municipality."
[8] *The Canadian Statesman*, 8 June 1966.
[9] *The Canadian Statesman*, 11 August 1976.
[10] *The Canadian Statesman*, 27 September 1961.
[11] *The Canadian Statesman*, 9 May 1962.

[12] The antipathy between the north and south wards dates back to the 19th century. As reported in *The Statesman* on 11 December 1873, "In one thing the South Warders are not far astray; if their cows can't roam at large they don't want residents of other Wards to roam into the South Ward seeking honours." North warders had stated their own feelings about loose cows in a 25 July 1872 issue of *The Statesman*, "Would you be kind enough to inform me by whose authority one man can pasture his cow in the Drill Shed Grounds, to the annoyance of all who may chance to go there for amusement. Surely the man who would put his cow in Public Grounds of that kind has no regard for his fellows." Not until 1898 was a bylaw passed prohibiting the running at large of cows. South warders did not quickly forget the calumny of that decision.

[13] *The Canadian Statesman*, 5 October 1966.

[14] Prepared by the students of The Division of Town and Regional Planning, School of Architecture, University of Toronto, *Official Plan for the Town of Bowmanville*, 1962.

[15] *The Canadian Statesman*, 14 March 1962.

[16] *The Canadian Statesman*, 14 March 1962.

[17] Ibid

Chapter Thirteen

The Town Which Nobody Leaves

"Bowmanville Jobs are Family Affairs/Town Which Nobody Leaves"
headlines on Bowmanville from
– *The Toronto Telegram*, 11 August 1951

"Thick description refers to a dense accumulation of ordinary information about a culture, as opposed to abstract or theoretical analysis."
– Broyard in *Prairyerth* by William Least-Heat Moon

"The transformation of the family man from a responsible member of society, interested in all public affairs, to a "bourgeois" concerned only with his private existence and knowing no civic virtue, is an international modern phenomenon."
– Hannah Arendt, *Organized Guilt and Universal Responsibility*

On the eve of Bowmanville's disappearance as a politically distinct entity the day after 31 December 1973, it would be revealing to know the attitudes and concerns of its citizens. The absence of time machines and inadequate local record-keeping would normally conceal such revelation.

Fortunately we have Robert Agger's "*Cross-National Community Study of Civic Involvement: Some Empirical Findings and Notes Towards a Theory*"[1] based on the survey of five communities of roughly comparable size (about 7,000 population) undertaken in the spring of 1969. These included Trzic, Slovenia (Yugoslavia); Konjic, Bosnia; Horice, Bohemia (Czechoslovakia); St. Helens, Oregon; and Bowmanville, Ontario.

Agger, a professor in the Department of Political Science at Hamilton's McMaster University, managed a study to "…help adult educators and other interested persons better perform functions of increasing active participation by citizens in their community politics as at least a partial means of developing increasingly participatory democracy or self-management or socialist consciousness and productive performance in the larger national polity."[2]—a mouthful indeed, but one with revealing observations.

The study notes in beginning that "…apart from a post second world war immigration of new Canadians from Holland (contributing about 10-15 % of the current population) recent arrivals to Bowmanville have been substantially religiously and ethnically homogeneous Protestant of English speaking Canadian backgrounds."[3]

According to Agger, the Dutch contribute a special character to the town by virtue of, what he termed, "their relatively fundamentalist" churches and separate school. Yet he also noted that their willingness to involve themselves in local affairs and their general economic well-being bred a certain resentment among long time residents "…who occasionally will speak of the 'Dutchies' as 'pushy'."[4]

Agger's study attributed a certain elitism in civic affairs and local politics to older established families descended from United Empire Loyalists (UEL) stock. Yet this seems excessive particularly since even the earliest arrivals were suspect UELs, having arrived long after the first wave and amidst a second phase driven more by economics and land owning possibilities. He was closer to the mark in noting that "…even Bowmanvillers who have been residents for twenty years are still 'newcomers'."[5]

Agger described the changing political climate of the town, suggesting that the local newspaper publisher and museum board members both had interests aligned with "old-timers" and various old families. These generally translated into federal and provincial political involvement while local politics fell to newer residents. Local politics among these people tended to be regional in focus rather than the immediate community and this may explain the relatively benign response to fundamental political change such as regional government.

The departure of Bowmanville's municipal independence and its amalgamation into the larger political unit of "The Town of Newcastle" as one of eight

Bowmanville High School Senior Rugby Team, Central Ontario Champions, 1940–41 school year.

area jurisdictions within the Region of Durham beginning in 1974, nevertheless left the old town with a still significant local political clout. As significant, however, was the role of *The Canadian Statesman* newspaper which, it has been suggested, was for many the real symbol of their local affiliation. In 1969 Agger found that the paper was read by the "...vast majority of Bowmanvillers...here was the central and most comprehensive source of news about local affairs. A study some 13 years earlier had indicated that the names of as many as 85% of the town's permanent citizens have appeared in the paper over a relatively short period. With growth probably came a lowering of such a figure, but the localistic character of the paper had been vigorously maintained."[6]

Analyzing the paper's content between 1967 and 1969, the study revealed that provincial matters were significantly less important than either local or federal political issues, and that generally there were few criticisms of local officials or notables. Industrial growth (it mattered not whether Canadian owned or American), was seen not only as the solution to most problems of unemployment and welfare, but as even more favourable than new housing which tended to distort assessment and tax revenue. This may explain the relatively late start Bowmanville had in attracting significant new residential construction in the booming greater Toronto region.

The study revealed a "...more participatory structure of civic roles" in Bowmanville than in the American community and that Bowmanville's important civic leadership roles were "more open and less elite in character than St. Helens despite the tradition of the UEL...", suggesting again that the original settlement of Bowmanville had only limited impact on the town's eventual development.

Significantly, while participant activity in association life (ranging from sports through adult education to civic affairs) not surprisingly followed general class, income and education levels of citizens, there was interest in these matters among all levels. Again this suggested the high degree of community cohesion and a belief in the possibility of action even if it was not always rewarded for certain groups.

The Agger study is as revealing for the composition of citizens interviewed. Of the 324 surveyed 281 were men as a result of the academics interest in "heads of household", a distinction which itself speaks to social changes since then. 45% of them had lived in Bowmanville for over twenty years and only 21% for five years or less.

The community's homogeneity was demonstrated by survey results indicating 88% of them were Protestant and 8% Catholics. Forty-eight percent were from blue collar homes and 25% from farms. Thirty-eight percent had at best an elementary school education and only 25% had graduated from or gone beyond high school. It was in short a blue collar community in which at the time young men in particular could expect to find line jobs at General Motors

The 4th Annual Lion's Club Minstrel Show held March 1953 in the upstairs Opera House of the Bowmanville Town Hall. What can one say about this bizarre photo except that it represents a fortunately vanished entertainment. Front row centre in tux and no makeup - Bob Kent

in Oshawa, Goodyear in Bowmanville or any of the other six major industries in the area. Perhaps not surprisingly 25% had changed their job at least once in the past five years.

What did the people of Bowmanville think on the eve of municipal change? Fully 65% said their family situation had changed for the better in the past five years and only 12% said it had got worse. Eighty-five percent were either somewhat or very satisfied with their standard of living. Asked whether they had adequate opportunities to develop their abilities and interests in their community 75% of Bowmanvillers responded positively in contrast to 61% in the Oregon and Yugoslavian community, 51% in the Bohemian community, and 35% in the Bosnian. In light of the volcano which later disrupted life in St. Helen's, the political turmoil and civil war in Yugoslavia and Bosnia, and the political uncoupling of the Czech Republic and Slovakia, one suspects this measure of satisfaction might be even more pronounced today.

In 1969 only a small proportion (19%) of those in Bowmanville were ready to move if they had the opportunity and just under 50% said no to a move under any circumstances. When all were asked if they would move to another community very similar to this one if they could get more than 50% increase in income, a remarkable 39% said they would not move at all. The authors, in somewhat deadpan fashion, said life in Bowmanville was "...satisfactory and pleasant" that it "...resembles more nearly many rural small towns of Ontario than a city of heavy immigration with mixed ethnic and religious groups."[7]

We can paint several different pictures of Bowmanville from the above description. Firstly the survey was biased in terms of male respondents defining their relationship to local woman in a particularly dominant, and to us now, somewhat offensive fashion. Did the women in those male-led households share the feeling of community well-being? And the social and ethnic cohesion might be read as well as a sign of implied bigotry. The study did reveal at least some mixed feeling towards the Dutch arrivals after World War Two a group whose culture was only marginally dissimilar.

But, in fairness, Bowmanville in 1969 was not too different from any other Ontario community of the period. And its unity of purpose and social compatibility were worthy achievements by themselves.

Notes

1 Robert Agger, *A Cross-National Community Study of Civic Involvement: Some Empirical Findings and Noted Towards a Theory*. (Hamilton: Department of Political Science, McMaster University, undated).
2 Ibid
3 Ibid
4 Ibid
5 Ibid
6 Ibid
7 Ibid

Chapter Fourteen

If It Sticks to Its Principles

*"We discover in the world, that our worst fears are unfulfilled;
yet we must fear, in order that we may feel delight."*
– Peter Ackroyd, *English Music*

*"The suburb is the last word in privatization, perhaps even
its lethal consummation, and it spells the end of authentic
civic life."*
– Andres Duany and Elizabeth Plater-Zyberk

*"Living in a cartoon landscape of junk architecture,
monotonous suburbs, ravaged countryside and trashed cities,
Americans sense that something is wrong. Our discontent is
expressed in phrases like "the loss of community" and "no
sense of place". Yet the issue of how we live is strikingly absent
from the debate about national problems, especially our
economic predicament."*
– James Howard Kunstler, "Zoned for Destruction,"
New York Times, 9 August 1993

"You can't eat scenery."
– a line from the movie *Local Hero*

Ｎational Geographic magazine's June 1996 focus on Toronto included a map of the province of Ontario complete with historical overview. Little communities like Bethany, Pontypool, Wesleyville and Omemee (the place that inspired singer Neil Young's lament for a town in north Ontario in his song "Helpless") appeared. Bowmanville which reached 23,000 residents that year (a growth of over 7,000 in five years) did not. It has been replaced by the historically suspect Clarington.

Old-timers had long feared the disappearance of Bowmanville's identity particularly after the amalgamation of the old townships of Darlington and Clarke with the town of Bowmanville and villages of Orono and Newcastle following the implementation of regional government in 1974.

The choice of Newcastle as name for this new political jurisdiction, one of eight in the Region of Durham immediately to the east of metropolitan Toronto, was not without some local anger. Newcastle was by most neutral accounts a perfectly reasonable choice. It was the name of the old District within which this part of Upper Canada was situated in the early part of the

The evolving main street around the turn of the century.

19th century before the reform of municipal government and the political ascendance of townships and counties. And while in the newly designated town it was also the name of a smaller community of about 2,000 residents[1] about five miles east of Bowmanville, that village arguably had more notable native sons. Daniel Massey had founded a famous Canadian farm implement business and sired a family that included a future Hollywood star and a governor general. As well, Joseph Atkinson had made *The Toronto Star* one of the great North American dailies. Of some small note, my laptop provides the name of Newcastle among its spell check words. It is silent on Bowmanville.

None of this however appeased the citizens of Bowmanville who felt aggrieved that their town had been ignored. Furthermore, while it retained a political representation in the ward structure created for the new municipal jurisdiction, many of its historic features such as its own police force disappeared. Indeed it might be said that Bowmanville stepped out of history on 1 January 1974 when its 116 year history as a distinct municipality ended.

Other places like Venice, whose seven hundred years of independence concluded with Napoleon's arrival in 1802, survived quite nicely after their political heritage was shattered, but for Bowmanville the verdict is still to be read. To give some sense of the small dislocation this change occasioned I recall an occurrence in the early fall of 1974. We had visitors from Toronto who left our apartment in Bowmanville and drove west for approximately ten miles into downtown Oshawa looking for pizza. Unlike Venice, Bowmanville in 1974, despite its nearly 12,000 residents, was remarkably short of Italian fast food.

King Street in the mid-century.

My friends would have a traumatic return. In the words of Rod Serling, they were about to enter a kind of twilight zone. Road maps had not as yet recognized the new region and they showed Bowmanville located about half way between Oshawa and the small village of Newcastle. Reaching the suburban outskirts of Oshawa as they drove back along Highway 2 they were confronted with a sign declaring their entry into the Town of Newcastle in the new Region of Durham. Looking at their map they noted that Newcastle was of course farther than they wanted to go and so turned back only to confront almost immediately a sign welcoming them to Oshawa. Clearly Bowmanville was not only too big to be circumscribed by such a short distance, but there should have been plenty of countryside between the two signs. Bowmanville had apparently disappeared.

Bowmanville's older citizens, people like Bob Kent, lobbied for years for a name change. In the process they kept the name of Bowmanville alive especially among new arrivals in the community which by 1991 had swollen to around 15,800. Finally they were granted a referendum whose wording appealed to the sense of grievance without suggesting a parcel of new names that might have been even more objectionable.[2]

Citizens of the Town of Newcastle did not so much vote for a new name as they narrowly rejected the old one by providing the municipality with their approval to consider other alternatives. A committee of residents from around the entire Town realized almost immediately however that calling this huge territory Bowmanville would be a kind of perverse negation of Bowmanville's own past by falsely identifying it with unaffiliated communities, people and land far beyond its historic reach. They were not, however, going to let their fellow citizens have a second chance to perhaps reluctantly, given the alternatives, vote to retain the Newcastle name. By combining the old township names of Darlington and Clarke, but in reverse order to the way people had once listed them, the committee came up with the perfectly horrible name of Clarington.

This seemed to satisfy the concerned citizens of Bowmanville though it shouldn't have. Where for almost twenty years these people had maintained a local identity by their antipathy to the Newcastle name, now this shallow moniker of Clarington aroused neither passion or anger.

New arrivals to the expanding suburbs of Bowmanville are inclined to think of themselves as citizens of the Municipality of Clarington and no one is concerned anymore to tell them otherwise. Bob Kent died shortly after the name change and I'm not sure he'd be happy to know his old hometown's name has perhaps never been more vulnerable. Even the venerable *Canadian Statesman* bills itself as "Clarington's community newspaper since 1854", having dropped reference to Bowmanville from its masthead.[3]

As important as a name is for identity, it is but one factor of many in defining a place for the people who live there. What shapes Bowmanville's future is significant population growth that has followed the construction of sewer and

Town Hall and Post Office, symbols of the Brick Town. The Post Office building is gone but the Town Hall in the foreground has been restored to serve the Municipality of Clarington in which Bowmanville is located. Note as well the line of trees on Temperance Street providing a model for future development.

water services. Draft changes to the Durham Region Official Plan projected a population of 95,000 for Bowmanville by the year 2021.[4]

The town had seen such estimates of major growth before and they had not materialized. A twenty year process however began in 1975 with the designation of a municipal area for Bowmanville encompassing the lands south of concession three to the lake and bound on the west by Highway 57 and in the east including the old lot 5 of Darlington Township.[5] It culminated with the Golden Report's findings in 1996 that linked areas such as Bowmanville into the Greater Toronto Region. These, in combination with almost daily work on road widenings and extension of municipal services, seemed to guarantee that the old goal of a greater Bowmanville was attainable.

The danger in such changes had been bluntly detailed as early as December 1972. The province of Ontario announced plans for a regional government stretching from the Scarborough boundary to Haldimand Township east of Cobourg largely to halt sprawl to the immediate east. Sprawl is a term hardly mentioned today, but suggests a desire to retain the distinctiveness of urban and rural areas. According to Gardiner Church, a planner in the Regional Government Organization Branch of the province's department of Treasury, Economics and Inter-governmental Affairs, the purpose was to protect the area between Port Hope-Cobourg and Oshawa from development pressures.

According to Church as quoted in a Pollution Probe report released in 1974, "...planners zeroed in on Clarke and Darlington townships in particular. We looked at the assessment base, and it became clear that there was no way that Clarke or Darlington could resist the blandishments of any developer. They were faced with the dilemma of increasing costs and a decreasing assessment base."[6]

The solution was the enhancement of the two centres on either side of Darlington-Clarke as "poles of growth" to counter the possibility of shoddy development on the fringe of an Oshawa-centred region. Immediately developers in the Bowmanville area objected because of potential limits on their activity. Citizens of Port Hope and Cobourg, fearing a projected population of 200,000 by the year 2000, also protested the designation and were able to get their areas deleted from the plans. Their proposal for a single tier government incorporating the old Northumberland and Durham Counties went nowhere however, as did a proposal for a regional government incorporating the Great Pine Ridge whose western boundary would be the town line between Darlington and Clarke. Bowmanville, in the middle of Darlington Township, and the largely rural area of Courtice on the edge of Oshawa, would be left to their own devices in countering the forces of urban sprawl.

What had been the old townships of Darlington and Clarke along with Bowmanville were incorporated into the regional government of Durham in 1974, but it would be almost twenty years before the development Church feared would actually be noticeable. By then however, the old historic connection with Northumberland County to the east and in particular Port Hope and Cobourg had faded as Bowmanville's citizens saw themselves increasingly a part of the greater Toronto area.

In 1997 there remained one last significant political connection between Bowmanville and its eastern neighbours—the Northumberland and Clarington (formerly Northumberland and Newcastle) Board of Education. Surprisingly this structure was retained in 1997 as the Province opted to realign the full Board with that of Peterborough. It had been previously anticipated that Clarington would be divorced from Northumberland County and lumped with the Durham Board of Education to conform with regional political boundaries.

Uncritical Acceptance of Growth

In Bowmanville the uncritical acceptance of growth found its greatest expression in the town's excitement at the construction of the world's largest nuclear facility a few miles southwest of town in the 1970s. This was a time when virtually every community in North America was protesting unwelcome modern intrusions, be they expressways or half way houses. A nuclear plant was perhaps the ultimate symbol of this intrusive presence and the lack of scientific and technological ability to mediate and in some cases even understand the impact of such facilities justified the anxiety.

Why was Bowmanville so compliant? It may be explained by the collapse of Bowmanville's grand ambitions of the 19th century when the town believed that it could compete with larger centres and even carve a significant economic hinterland for itself through the construction of railways and attraction of major industries. One thing that those without a historical appreciation forget is that most issues and problems are recurrent and that a survey of newspapers over a long period will reveal a tremendous synchronicity of opinions and challenges. For almost all of the 20th century, Bowmanville has wrestled with its frustration at the loss of what it once envisioned itself to be.

This unwavering support for more growth continued well into the 1990s. At a meeting to review population targets in 1990 most participants stressed the need for even greater incentives and land allocation for urban growth. One Bowmanville resident said the proposed expansion of living areas for the town was constructive but conservative. Jane Pepino, a lawyer representing the Northbrook Development Group owning land north of Concession three and west of Liberty Street, asked that the northern area be considered for growth.[7]

"She said the area can be serviced," *The Statesman* reported, "and suggested without its inclusion in the plan, the municipality could have difficulties meeting its target population."[8] There were requests as well to increase the commercial floor space—a desire consistent with development west of Bowmanville along Highway 2.

No one was reported to have even mildly questioned the entire ideology of growth. Historically *The Statesman* and town leaders had accepted the philosophy of expansion less from any interest in the obvious financial benefit accruing to out of town developers than a kind of splendidly naive belief that any change was beneficial. Boosterism of this sort contrasts dramatically with European models where hundreds of years of experience have allowed for a mature respect for the separation of town and country. In Europe however such separation has been purchased at a cost. Retailers on main street are protected from competitors on the edge of town and so sale price is high and choice is often limited.

Until the 1990s Bowmanville was more a classic European town than anything comparable in North America. So extreme however was the official antipathy to this rather unique and favoured position that one local employee boasted that while no fast food restaurants existed when he arrived in the 1980s, a few years later six were in place.

Yet ambivalence towards new development continued to characterize local opinion in the mid 1990s. This was demonstrated by a request for clearly differentiated space at the point where Scugog and Middle roads divide in the town's northwest, and the appeal by a rural landowner on Lamb's Road for some form of separation between his rose business and a new housing development.

Special land uses on Bowmanville's periphery have contributed to the community's character. Among these are Mostert's Greenhouses on Lamb's Road and the Bowmanville Zoo on Highway 2, east of Mearns Avenue. Yet in April 1996 The Schickendanz Brothers development company requested that property near these businesses be included within the Bowmanville urban area and designated for residential and related uses. It was reported that municipal planning staff recommended approving the amendment since it "generally conforms." [9]

For Richard Mostert, a grower of roses for local florists, development threatened his dependence on two shallow wells, while street lights "...would make it difficult for some plants to grow." [10] New houses also posed problems of vandalism and theft. Mostert requested that the present greenbelt be maintained.

Bowmanville Zoo's owners warned that private urban zoos in other parts of the world were nearing extinction. "To our knowledge," said Zoo director, Michael Hackenberger, "there is only one other situation like that enjoyed in Bowmanville and that exists in Hamburg, Germany." [11] Residential development would potentially harm the elephant breeding centre and prompt daredevils to invade the area housing lions, tigers, and wolves. "We're not opposed to development," he said, "but we must safeguard and protect the zoo site." [12]

Meanwhile in the northwest corner of Bowmanville in an area which for years had seemed almost like a small nearby village, massive development was finally overwhelming the local residents. In defense they asked that a park be located at the Y-shaped parcel of land between Middle and Scugog roads. A closer examination of their concerns however revealed a narrowly protective

Downtown promotions take many forms.

desire to stop a ten unit subdivision intended for those who could only afford a semi-detached home in favour of a smaller three to five unit subdivision.[13]

There was real pain however in the fear of one resident that Clarington was going the way of Pickering and Ajax. No one mentioned Bowmanville. It was said that the development would destroy the woods which were home to animals, birds and flora. "We're not against progress or the building of homes," they said, "but feel there is a need for boundaries."[14] They were told however that the proposed population density was within guidelines.

Similarly in attempting to ameliorate the impact of new retail development on Bowmanville's fringe, the former Town of Newcastle had supported plans to provide at least some form of visual connection and identity between proposed development on Highway 2 and that of the older business core of Bowmanville. Council told Zellers that they should build a facility which fronted on the street with parking hidden in the back. According to an editorial in the 8 May 1993 *Oshawa Times*, the company used "…their financial muscle to blackmail council."[15] *The Times* reported that the mayor appeared willing to cave in to the developer's request for a traditional strip mall development and not one intended to preserve and extend Bowmanville's downtown with new development of architectural value and consistent appearance.

The Oshawa Times editorial angrily declared, "Newcastle doesn't have to do whatever Zellers or Markborough Properties tells it to. Bowmanville is one of the richest little towns in Canada—a community of home-owning, two-car, two-income families. Zellers investment in the community is not dependent on trashing the town's plans with another ugly strip mall destined to get uglier as time goes by. Zellers interest in Bowmanville is predicated on the market, not the parking. Zellers needs markets like Bowmanville, and [Mayor Diane] Hamre can play hardball with the chain."

"If Newcastle caves in to demands for strip malls, it will get exactly what it bargained for—second-rate, penny-ante, ugly development, and limited opportunities for first-class developers who are looking for a first-class environment for their investments."[16]

With real passion, the editorial, noted that many small towns had flourished by preserving their history and character. "Bowmanville has that same opportunity. If it sticks to its principles it could attract investment that will sustain itself for generations. Or it could become an anonymous little tract that reproduces the ambience of Ellesmere Road in Scarborough."[17] Three years later Zellers received approval to construct a compromise facility—one that no longer protected the vision of Bowmanville's downtown streetscape.

On a related issue the mayor and council who had generally supported most types of development spoke of the disaster that would follow the building of retail warehouses.[18] Bowmanville's downtown would be killed if these types of stores were allowed, Mayor Hamre said. One councillor however said if such warehouses were not allowed then they would locate in nearby municipalities.

The residents of Bowmanville had an opportunity to express their ideas on the community in a survey conducted by a private research organization Collis and Reed in 1994.[19] The survey followed the existing political boundaries of the municipality in which Ward 1 defined the western part (the old Darlington Township) including Courtice, Ward II encompassed Bowmanville, and Ward III the eastern part or the old township of Clarke.

Opinions differed radically amongst these areas. For instance only 2% of Bowmanville residents complained of high taxes, the dominant mantra of the provincial government elected in 1995, in contrast to 16 and 19% in the rural areas. Yet in contrast to a high number of rural dwellers who found open space the most significant element of their lifestyle, 46% of Bowmanville citizens said that the small town atmosphere of Clarington was the most important feature of the municipality. Bowmanville residents were concerned about the lack of stores and businesses. Most significantly they were against too much residential development in their community. Improving the business environment was the most important objective for the municipality.

Well might they have had trepidation about this new growth which, as typified in one *Toronto Sun* advertisement of September 1996, showed a bowler and the headline "Bowmanville for Dollars"[20]—a tasteless and somewhat pointless invocation to buy a house in the Apple Blossom community of Bowmanville (though Bowmanville does have a proud bowling heritage).

Downtown sidewalk sale.

What might this all mean? As they indicated in a comprehensive survey in the late sixties, Bowmanville citizens believed in the need to preserve the quality of life in their community by matching residential to commercial and industrial growth. Dragged into the Toronto region and its systemic growth, they nevertheless defended the historic integrity of their community.

In 1996 the Municipality of Clarington brought forward a local political redistribution which incorporated four wards. One respected the old township of Clarke, but the others divided the old township of Darlington by a north-south alignment in which the Holt Road separated the first ward, and Liberty Street became the dividing line for wards two and three stretching from Lake Ontario back to the tenth concession. Bowmanville had lost its last form of distinct representation and even if two residents of Bowmanville proper were elected their responsibility, orientation, and vision would have to be for a greater geographic area which owed little to the urban distinctiveness of Bowmanville.[21]

Bowmanville, according to *National Geographic* magazine, had lost its cartographic recognition. Under regional government it had been deprived of its unique political identity by its subservience within the Town of Newcastle. And now within Clarington, Bowmanville had become a subdivided political territory aligned with areas with which it has little in common in the way of town versus country living. The urban reality of Bowmanville had become but a minor piece of well-developed real estate. Its future and its planning would focus not on its unique features, character or history, but simply its place within a larger, yet to be realized, environment.

The Official Plan

The official plan for the Municipality of Clarington released in 1996 is generous in its regard for the quality of life, sustainability of the environment, and protection of cultural heritage. It is a less harsh version of the future and respectful of the rights of First Nations, and the preservation of streetscapes of cultural, historic and/or architectural significance.

But it also divorces these features from the everyday reality of the municipality. As well Bowmanville has become no more than a populated setting within a larger planning framework. It is as if the town as a distinct entity had ceased to exist and instead has been replaced by a collection of neighbourhood planning units made up of the following populations:

Northglen:	3,400
Knox :	5,400
Fenwick:	5,500
Brookhill:	5,100
Elgin:	4,000
Apple Blossom:	4,800
Vincent Massey:	4,400
East Main Central Area:	2,800
Memorial:	4,000
Waverly:	4,000
Westvale:	4,800
West Main Central Area:	3,700
Darlington Green:	2,600
Central:	2,000
Port Darlington:	3,200

This targeted population of 59,700 lowered earlier projections, but the vision of a series of one-dimensional residential enclaves with little idea of urban amenities such as mixed uses and retail integration suggested a largely suburban vision. Some new communities, like that based around Elephant Hill in the north east part of Bowmanville, are fortunate to have special natural features such as a rolling topography to give them character. In the absence of community centres or small shops the orientation of the entire residential area around baseball diamonds is a peculiar though pleasing and quirky local feature.

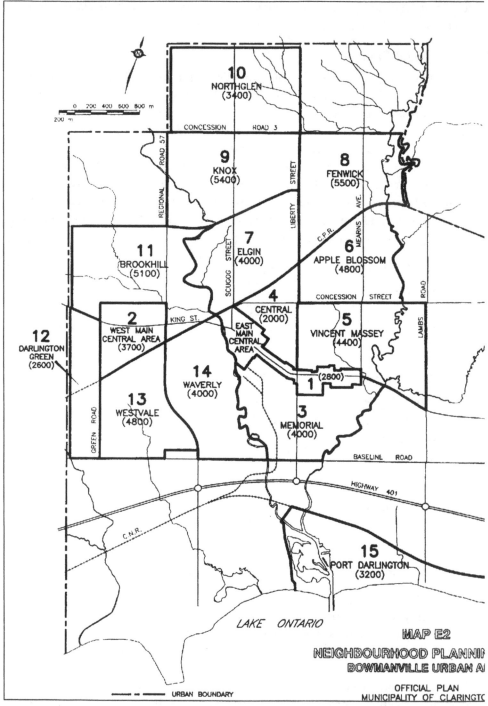

1996 Neighbourhood Planning Units for Bowmanville Urban Area Municipality of Clarington.

It seems to be an unplanned celebration of two Blue Jay World Series victories which occurred around the same time as construction.

Cultural heritage planning in the Official Plan focused only on the past built environment, and its preservation or recognition was reserved for designated areas. In this vision the "…heritage downtown of Bowmanville…" as well as the Lake Ontario waterfront and Oak Ridges Moraine had become a kind of living museum.

It does not appear that these areas will be used as guides or exemplars, for future development consistent with the evolved character of the town. Bowmanville is threatened with becoming a kind of irrelevant old museum surrounded by new areas of suburban development paying limited heed to ideas of a reinvigorated urbanism. There is however some refreshing discussion espoused by town planners about a mixed urbanity of integrated land uses such as the placement of a variety store on a street of houses as can be found on Second Street between Elgin and Prospect streets in the old north end. As well there is support for a grid-like pattern of streets encouraging pedestrian activity and connection between neighbourhoods as in Bowmanville's existing core.

In the private sector there were small though significant signs of encouragement such as a Kaitlin development, Clarington Corners, which promised siding in a variety of colours, wood trim, pillars and porches, garages flush with the front of the houses, and in some cases garages in a lane at the rear. Its isolation, however, from other parts of the Aspen Springs development to emphasize its heritage styling once again suggested a vision of character and history divorced from everyday application in all features of Bowmanville's future.

Designing a Future Bowmanville

It is unclear whether the political and public will exists to enhance the small signs of renewed town life consistent with a "new urbanism." To date Bowmanville has started upon a course of false urban development which rejects the principles of street life and variety, fails to differentiate sharply between town and country, and replicates a suburban growth style in which local character and identity is replaced by the ideals of consumerism and lack of unique features that would say, "this is Bowmanville."

The issue in designing the future of communities is not preserving some quaint idea of the small town as a place where you can leave your doors unlocked and everyone knows your name. There can be ugliness and sadness in the small town as well as the large. In early 1996 a little girl at Central school in Bowmanville was murdered by her stepfather. A small town history might not report such matters and may even attempt to deny tragedy, but it shouldn't. They are part of the community's life which is as often brutal and tragic as it can be glorious and beautiful.

The life and character of the small town like the very large city against which it is often juxtaposed is actually not a case of either/or. Both in fact share more than the pieces that separate them. Both at their best are places of vitality with their own strengths and special features. The big city be it London or Paris, New York or Toronto is a place with many different people and events occurring within its boundaries. It attracts wonderful entertainment, street life, and the ability to enjoy much within walking distance or through public transit.

A small town likewise is marked by the everyday mixture of many different land uses in which one can walk to the library, town hall or local businesses, all of which are magnificent because, and not in spite, of their ordinariness. And walking is the constant feature. In the case of the small town its glory is the ability to walk from almost any point in the town into the country within a time period of no more than fifteen minutes.

Between these two allies of human settlement are the present tracts of one-use territories in which houses, businesses, and libraries all have their distinctive place reachable in any realistic assessment only by car. They are the features of a particular cultural bias towards the protection of the private.

The proper vision for the next century looks askance at ungainly impersonal wooden fences which have begun to front major street thoroughfares in Bowmanville. It builds on the model of existing Bowmanville streetscapes and their curious mixture of odd land parcels carved out by the entwining of a rigid north-south grid with main roads passing at an angle to them and by which neighbourhoods are linked. It mixes land uses by designing new retail and work areas within new developments. Road widenings are discouraged and instead strategies are implemented for calming traffic and encouraging the pedestrian. It is quixotic and intentional like the wonderful new ballparks in America which borrow from old design areas and introduce the best and most urbanely pleasing of new technology.

At the root of any desirable future is an appreciation for the existing built environment and its enhancement in new development. Each list of what should be preserved is obviously personal and so the author begins by noting some of those uniquely defined and often quirky features emerging from nearly two centuries of history. These include:

- the line of trees visible on the horizon as one walks east along Carlisle Ave.
- the farm on a distant hill as one looks east from the beer store
- the bend in the road where Middle and Scugog Road intersect, like the choice between two paths one might take in life
- the sense of village life on the Scugog Road west of this intersection with its two Dutch Christian schools
- the line of trees and occasional train on the bridge as one looks west along Highway 2 from the four corners
- Bowmanville's own island, a small piece of land surrounded by the Bowmanville Creek just south of the old Vanstone millpond

- the crosstown freeway where the entry lane onto Highway 401 at Liberty Street combines with the exit lane from Highway 401 to Waverley Road
- the Bowmanville subway, an unused rail line running parallel to Hunt Street
- the annual homemade ice rinks on the Strike (site of the annual "world" ball hockey on ice championships) and Hoy lawns on Beech and Concession streets
- the sound of a train whistle from the CPR track running through the north end of town by the ghost of the old CPR Station
- the layout of town streets running on a north-south axis to Highway 2 which cuts diagonally across Bowmanville
- the Soper Creek baseball diamond with an outfield of creek and magnificent trees
- the eastern entrance into Bowmanville along Concession Street past apple orchards and the former training school, and down into the new subdivisions
- the western entrance into Bowmanville down a hill on the Base Line Road
- an 1870s litho of Bowmanville in which the shape of the downtown, church steeples and the Vanstone Mill can still be seen today
- the upper stories of buildings on the south side of main street west of the four corners
- the fabulous old Oak tree on Beech Avenue once said to be an Indian meeting place and a model for future tree planting
- Central School and its 1889 origin date on the building mantle
- the Rotary Park entrance into the Bowmanville Creek valley at the base of Temperance Street
- the bend in the row of houses on Galbraith Court southeast of the high school
- the 19th century designation as the "brick town" still reflected in the many fine old brick buildings
- the many television/movie productions using Bowmanville as a backdrop, the multitude of video outlets, the ratio of one cinema for each 2,000 residents, and the movie star animal residents of the local Zoo, making Bowmanville the "movie town"
- the great 19th century ball team, the Bowmanville Royal Oaks
- the local cemetery, where Mr. Climie and Mr. Cubitt, two 19th century rivals, are buried within a stone's throw of each other, and a monument to Fred Higginbotham (only Bowmanville citizen to play on a Stanley Cup winner) donated by the Winnipeg Victorias hockey club
- *The Canadian Statesman* newspaper, Bowmanville's own unique newspaper since the 1850's

- Bowmanville's barn-like five pin bowling alley on the Base Line
- Lovers Lane, a narrow and wonderful street which forces cars to slow down
- Port Darlington Harbour area recently linked to the Waterfront Trail stretching from Hamilton to Trenton
- the lost sounds and sights of the town from the factory whistle of the Dominion Organ Factory to the Ontario Bank building
- local tastes and smells from Hanc's chip wagon to burning leaves
- The former boys' reformatory on Concession Street, now St. Stephen's Catholic High School, but once a Prisoner of War Camp and site of the "Battle of Bowmanville" where German officers protested prisoner shackling and from which Peter Krug escaped in April 1942 [22]

Enhancing or re-introducing these features would create a place which is more than just another suburban enclave of a greater Toronto region. In so doing something of the landscape, the small town flavour, the local landmarks and people, and the other distinct touches will remain and inform at least a partial identity for new development.

Symbol of the Bowmanville Business Area, established to promote the "Historic Downtown" and empowered under provincial legislation to levy an additional tax on businesses in the area for commercial enhancement.

Far from blaming the private sector, the real fault has been what John van Nostrand has called the "…tendency to ignore those parts of …developments which were intended to accommodate the much more routine activities of the public-at-large—the streets, walkways, parks, schoolgrounds, meeting halls, transit lines, etc. These 'public parks' of the town, in that they constitute its public infrastructure, establish the physical territory within which patterns of identity either evolve or disappear. Consequently, it is within these areas that new patterns of urban re-identification will be created." [23] This is above all else a public enterprise by designating spaces and public life prior to the entry of developers and real estate agents. Private builders can then assume their proper place in meeting public specifications.

The most encouraging sign for the future health and identity of Bowmanville has been the virtual re-invention of Bowmanville's downtown under the leadership of the Bowmanville Business Centre. Facade studies and a 1991 community design analysis by the Ontario Association of Architects, have provided local business people with a renewed sense of community direction, pride and promotional opportunity. Annual events including the Maple Festival and Antique Show in May, the Apple Festival and Craft Sale in October, and the Christmas Tree Lighting ceremony in December, have provided new and old residents alike with a sense of local connection.

The task of all citizens is to imagine how Bowmanville's past, its present features and its future vision might be combined to create a vibrant townlife.

Notes

[1] Newcastle Village's 1971 census population was 1,942.

[2] Letter from Mayor Diane Hamre describing the name change process, 30 January 1995.

[3] Ironically back on 18 May 1983 *The Canadian Statesman* in an editorial entitled "Time to Correct Mistake," commented "This year, the non-existent Town of Bowmanville is celebrating its 125th anniversary although officially it ceased to exist 10 years ago. So, under present conditions we are in effect holding a celebration over a corpse, a memorial in essence. And that doesn't make much sense when Bowmanville is very much alive. We feel it's about time something was done to correct at least one of the mistakes made a decade ago. Surely it would be most appropriate this year to start the wheels turning to have the name of this town renamed Bowmanville, as should have happened at the time."

[4] "Noting that the plan calls for a population of 95,000 in Bowmanville and 60,000 in Courtice, whereas the town [Newcastle] prefers 75,000 and 40,000 respectively, [Newcastle Councillor John] O'Toole said, "I suggest that someone's not listening." from 12 May 1992, The Oshawa Times.

5 Municipal Planning Consultants, *District Plan Town of Newcastle District Planning Area*, 1975.

6 *Tail of the Elephant: A Guide to Regional Planning and Development in Southern Ontario.* (Toronto: Pollution Probe, 1974), p. 0.

7 *The Canadian Statesman*, 7 November 1990.

8 Ibid

9 *The Clarington Independent*, 4 May 1996.

10 Ibid

11 Ibid

12 Ibid

13 *The Canadian Statesman*, 8 May 1996.

14 Ibid

15 *The Oshawa Times*, 8 May 1993.

16 Ibid

17 Ibid

18 *Clarington This Week*, 9 June 1996.

19 *Attitudes of Clarington Residents*, Collis and Reed Research. (Bowmanville: 1974).

20 *The Sunday Sun*, 15 September 1996, p. HOMES 25.

21 *The Clarington/Courtice Independent*, 5 October 1996, p. 17.

22 John Melady, *Escape from Canada! The Untold Story of German POWs in Canada 1939-1945.* (Toronto: Macmillan, 1981).

23 *Will There Be Room for the Public*, private memo of John van Nostrand to Janet Moggridge, 4 April 1975.

24 Ontario Association of Architects, *Bowmanville, CAUSE (Community Assist for an Urban Study Effort)*, September 1991.

Photo Credits

Introduction

(a) This 1926 Ontario tourism map shows Bowmanville forty-two miles east of downtown Toronto on the north side of Lake Ontario. While the town hasn't moved, Toronto creeps ever closer.

(b) 1991 map of the ever-expanding Bowmanville showing the distinctive downtown layout along Highway 2 which cuts at a right angle across the grid. The town has since grown north, and westwards.

(c) Main Street Bowmanville, contemporary scenes from downtown Bowmanville on King Street (Highway 2)
Garth Gilpin Collection

(d) A Classic Photo of Bowmanville's Market Square, celebrating Queen Victoria's Diamond Jubilee, 24 May 1897
Bowmanville Museum

1. The Land is a Narrative

(101) Boys Skating on Vanstone Mill's Frozen Pond, 26 December 1916

Public Archives of Canada, Reference PA 70101

2. The Deed of Conveyance

(201) The Vanstone Pond and creek area, where fishing has provided an historic link between the original native population and the current residents.

3. The Building Blocks of Settlement

(301) The Four Corners of Bowmanville, at King and Temperance Streets, before 1900. The grid layout of streets and alignment of King Street (Highway 2) shaped the streetscape of Bowmanville. Town Hall is over stores in centre of picture, with Market Square, Fire Hall, and bandstand in background. People on street include (l.-r.), Mr. Horsey, Mr. Trebilcock, H. McCready, J.H. Jury, Jim McDonald, Harry Cann, Miss Medland (whose millinery store is in building on the right)

(302) A later view of the Four Corners, showing buildings which with the exception of the Town Hall in the background have now been demolished.

(303) Aerial view of Bowmanville.

4. Few More Picturesque Spots in Ontario

(401) Bowmanville from the west

(402) Bowmanville from the west along present Highway 2, c. 1905-10.
Garfield Shaw Collection, Bowmanville Museum

5. Our Bank

(501) Described as "the most beautiful commercial building in Bowmanville", the Ontario Bank building was demolished in 1971. Words fail to capture the ignominy of that action.
Garfield Shaw Collection, Bowmanville Museum

6. Genuine Original Men are Scarce

(601) Head shots of Frederick Cubitt, George Haines, Francis McArthur, and Robert R. Loscombe—four of the prominent Bowmanville personalities in this chapter, from "Picture the Way We Were".

(602) William Climie, Bowmanville's original "Statesman" and his successor Moses James.

(603) Train Arriving from East into Grand Trunk Railway Station, photo is c. 1910. VIA trains run on line today, but none stop in Bowmanville.
Garfield Shaw Collection, Bowmanville Museum

(604) One of First Three Automobiles in Town. A two cylinder McLaughlin Touring Car bought 12 June 1908 by Fred Foster.
Ontario Archives, Reference S-5197

(605) Businessmen in front of Frank Pethick's Barber Shop, 1910.(now 26

King Street West) from the left: Frank
Pethick, —, —, —, John B. Mitchell,
Harry Rice, —, *Canadian Statesman*
editor, Moses A. James
*Telephone Historical Collection, Bell
Canada, Reference 8529*

(606) William Climie's lasting legacy,
The Canadian Statesman
Garth Gilpin Collection

7. **Places of Grace**

(701) Four Bowmanville Friends, 1901.
back: Clarence Meath, Wallace Shaw
front: Alex Beith, Fred Downey
*Garfield Shaw Collection, Bowmanville
Museum*

(702) The Original "Senate" in the
card room above Cawkers Butcher
Shop around 1900
(l. - r.) Carl B. Kent, George Mason,
Fred Kidd, Bill Perrin (front), —
(back), Charles Blair (back standing),
Fred Manning, J.B. Mitchell, William
C.King, Charles Keith, W.F. Allen,
A.E. McLaughlin (standing), R.D.
Davidson (in front of McLaughlin),
Pete Garret (holding dog), Alan
William (standing), Thomas Fairbairn,
Jim Deyman (in front of Fairbairn),
John Moorecroft.

8. **Not Afraid to Face Public Opinion**
(801) Ada Hind portrait from 1884/85
period. Commanding officer for the
establishment of the Salvation Army in
Bowmanville in 1884, she served into
1886 and oversaw the building of the
Army's temple on King Street (on the
present day site of the Veltri Complex
east of Division Street).
*Garfield Shaw Collection, Bowmanville
Museum*

(802) An Early (1907) Casual Photo of
Two Bowmanville Women. Woman on
left is Florence Mayer, girl friend of the
photographer William Wesley Shaw
who left town to work in New York
City. She was daughter of a prominent
Bowmanville furrier, Markus Mayer.

The other woman is unknown.
*Garfield Shaw Collection, Bowmanville
Museum*

(803) Ladies Hockey Team (1924)
represented Bowmanville in
Lakeshore League
front (l. to r.) Hattie Seymour
Armstrong, Mildred Luxton
Edmondson, Nell Piper Wilson
back (l. to r.) Mansfield Cook, Maude
Wilcox Elford, Bessie Kilgannon
Donoghue, Alma Piper Cole, Nora
Cluff, Gladys Mutton, Gordon
Richards

(804) Nina Neads in the 1950s.
*Garfield Shaw Collection, Bowmanville
Museum*

9. **A Drowsy State of Existence**

(901) Turn of the Century in
Bowmanville (note the number of
bicycles popular in the 1890s)

(902) Dominion Organ and Piano
Factory Building, another lost
Bowmanville treasure
Garth Gilpin Collection

(903) Goodyear Rubber Works

(904) Staff of Goodyear's Hard Tires
Department (1922).
(l. to r.) George Raby, Ernie Jones,
Lyall Burden, Charles Smith,
—, Ben King, Joe Childs, E.
Woodward, Harry Westnutt, Alf
Richards (foreman)
*Garfield Shaw Collection, Bowmanville
Museum*

10. **The Lives of Ordinary People**

(1001) Central Public School in
Bowmanville, built in 1889 and still in
use today

(1002) Central Public School and
Bowmanville High School. Stu
Candler's two schools. The High
School is now located in a modern
building on Liberty Street.

(1003) Stuart Candler, last of the
millers at the Vanstone Mill stands in

the renovated building in 1982.
Garfield Shaw Collection, Bowmanville Museum

11. He Has done some Good in the Community

(1101) H.C. Tait's Camp on Bowmanville's beach at Lake Ontario, summer 1893. An image of the Bowmanville High School has been included on the side of the tent.
Garfield Shaw Collection, Bowmanville Museum

(1102) Bowmanville's own short wave radio station
Garfield Shaw Collection, Bowmanville Museum

(1103) Bowmanville Harbour

(1104) Famous World Long Distance Runner Alfred Shrubb and James Lake Morden meet in 1928. Morden brought Shrubb to Bowmanville to run the Cream of Barley Mill, camp, and park.
Garfield Shaw Collection, Bowmanville Museum

(1105) The Band of the Ontario Training School for Boys, parading on King Street near Temperance c. 1955-60, past the Ontario Bank (then occupied by the Bank of Montreal) building and the Post Office, now both demolished.
Garfield Shaw Collection, Bowmanville Museum

12. Town Landmark Gives Way to Community Progress

(1201) Digging up Main Street. Preparing to lay pipes for the first waterworks in Bowmanville, 1912-13. Balmoral (now Castle) Hotel is in the upper right of the photo.
Garfield Shaw Collection, Bowmanville Museum

(1202) Beech Avenue (incorrectly spelled as Beach). William C. King's house is shown in foreground with his daughter's income property and home next door.

(1203) Goodyear Tire and Rubber Company Staff, c. 1910-15
Garfield Shaw Collection, Bowmanville Museum

(1204) South side of King Street, 1946, just west of Temperance Street.
Garfield Shaw Collection, Bowmanville Museum

13. The Town Which Nobody Leaves

(1301) Bowmanville High School Senior Rugby Team, Central Ontario Champions, 1940-41.
back (l.-r.) Harry Jackman (coach), Harold Cashourn, Keith Slemon, Bill Brown, Brenton Rickard, S. Blain Elliott, Harold Longworth (coach), Mark Lambourne, Louis Densem, Bill Hutchinson, Sid Rundle, Don Venton, Louis Dippell (Principal)
front (l.-r.) Fred Payne, Don Allin, Ken Summersford, Lindsay Mitchell, Jack "Sandy" Colville, Carl Fisher, Horace "Bub" Moses, Alan Tamblyn, George Underhill, Alan Ferguson, Don Rowe. Absent: Gilbert McIlveen.
Garfield Shaw, Bowmanville Museum

(1302) The 4th Annual Lion's Club Minstrel Show held March 1953 in the upstairs Opera House of the Bowmanville Town Hall. What can one say about this bizarre photo except that it represents a fortunately vanished entertainment.
Front row centre in tux and no makeup - Bob Kent
Garfield Shaw Collection, Bowmanville Museum

14. If It Sticks to Its Principles

(1401) The Evolving Main Street around the turn of the century

(1402) A mid-century scene

(1403) Town Hall and Post Office, symbols of the Brick Town. The Post Office building is gone but the Town Hall in the foreground has been restored to serve the Municipality of

Clarington in which Bowmanville is
located. Note as well the line of trees
on Temperance Street providing a
model for future development.

(1404) Garth Gilpin Collection

(1405) A recent downtown sidewalk
sale promotion

(1406) 1996 Neighbourhood Planning
Units for Bowmanville Urban Area
Municipality of Clarington

(1407) Symbol of the Bowmanville
Business Area, established to promote
the "Historic Downtown" and empowered under provincial legislation to
levy an additional tax on businesses in
the area for commercial enhancement.

Appendix A

Bowmanville Population statistics (boundary changes have expanded original area)

1825:	118	Fairbairn
1827:	666	Fairbairn
1851:	1,650	Spelt
1861:	2,721	Fairbairn
1871:	3,034	Census
1881:	3,504	Census
1891:	3,377	Census
1901:	2,731	Census
1911:	2,814	Census
1921:	3,233	Census
1931:	4,080	Census
1941:	4,113	U of T
1951:	5,430	Spelt
1956:	6,634	U. of T.
1957:	6,906	U. of T.

1958:	7,112	U. of T.
1959:	7,203	U. of T.
1960:	7,308	U. of T.
1961:	7,397	Darlington Impact Study
1966:	8,513	Darlington Impact Study
1971:	8,947	Census
1975:	11,426	Darlington Impact Study
1976:	12,165	Planning Dept.
1981:	13,080	Planning Dept.
1986:	13,325	Planning Dept.
1991:	15,800	Planning Dept.
1994:	21,324	Planning Dept.
1995:	22,459	Planning Dept.
1996:	23,221	Planning Dept.

Appendix B

Bibliography

1. **Major Sources on Bowmanville**
   The Canadian Statesman newspaper available in the Bowmanville Branch of the Clarington Public Library and in various collections

   J.T. Coleman, **History of the Early Settlement of Bowmanville and Vicinity.** (Bowmanville: 1875)

   J.B. Fairbairn, **History and Reminiscences of Bowmanville.** (Bowmanville News Print, 1906)

   Hamlyn, Lunney, and Morrison, **Bowmanville: A Retrospect.** (Bowmanville Centennial Committee, 1958)

   Garfield Shaw et al., **Picture the Way We Were.** (Bowmanville: Mothersill, 1980)

   John Squair, **The Townships of Darlington and Clarke.** (Toronto: University of Toronto Press, 1927)

2. **Urban and Regional Planning Sources**
   Municipal Planning Consultants, **District Plan Town of Newcastle District Planning Area.** 1975

   Ontario Association of Architects, **Bowmanville, CAUSE (Community Assist for an Urban Study Effort).** September 1991

   Students of the Division of Town and Regional Planning, School of Architecture, University of Toronto, **Official Plan for the Town of Bowmanville.** (1962)

   Tail of the Elephant: A Guide to Regional Planning and Development in Southern Ontario. (Toronto: Pollution Probe, 1974)

3. **Additional Sources on Bowmanville**
   Robert Agger, **A Cross-National Community Study of Civic Involvement: Some Empirical**

   Findings and Notes Towards a Theory. (Hamilton: Department of Political Science, McMaster University, undated)

   Attitudes of Clarington Residents. Collis and Reed Research (Bowmanville: 1974)

   Edwin Chesterfield Coleman's diary excerpts as found in the Bowmanville Museum

   Falls, Hobson and Humber, **Central Public School 1889-1989 "A Centennial Celebration".**

   Hall and McCulloch, **Sixty Years of Canadian Cricket.** (Toronto: Bryant Printing, 1895)

   Heritage Walking Tour of Historic Bowmanville, **The Belvedere (Quarterly Journal of the Bowmanville Museum) No. 1.** (Bowmanville Museum: 1993)

   Historical Atlas of Northumberland and Durham Counties. (H. Belden and Co. 1878)

   Leo Johnson, **History of the County of Ontario 1615-1875.** (Whitby: Corporation of the County of Ontario, 1973)

   Sherrell Branton Leetooze, **The First 200 Years: A brief history of Darlington Township.** (Bowmanville: Lynn Michael-John Associates, 1994)

   John Melady, **Escape from Canada! The Untold Story of German POWs in Canada 1939-1945.** (Toronto: Macmillan, 1981)

   Clayton Morgan, Bommanville's Mysterious Electric Railway, **Bowmanville Downtowner.** Vol. 1 Issue 3, November 1994

   Official Opening of Rotary Park and Dedication of Colville Memorial Clock Tower Program, 2 June 1996

Shane Peacock, **The Great Farini: The High-Wire Life of William Hunt.** (Toronto: Viking, 1995)

Heather Robertson, **Driving Force: The McLaughlin Family and the Age of the Car.** (Toronto: McClelland and Stewart, 1996)

Two Centuries of Change: United Counties of Northumberland and Durham 1767-1967. (Cobourg: 1967)

George Vice, **The Post Office and Early Development in Bowmanville.** (Bowmanville: self-published, 1993)

various issues of The Belvedere (Quarterly Journal of the Bowmanville Museum): The Oshawa Times, Clarington This Week, Clarington Independent, The Toronto Globe, The Toronto Telegram, The Toronto Star

4. **Sources on the Ontario Landscape**

Blake and Greenhill, **Rural Ontario.** (Toronto: University of Toronto Press, 1969)

Edwin Guillet, **The Story of Canadian Roads.** (Toronto: University of Toronto Press, 1966)

Scott Little, **Main Street - Cobourg, Ontario.** Unpublished essay submitted in fulfilment of requirement for GGRC01Y at Scarborough College - University of Toronto, March 1978

Jacob Spelt, **Urban Development in South-Central Ontario.** (Toronto: McClelland and Stewart, 1972)

George W. Spragge, The Districts of Upper Canada 1788-1849, **Ontario History XXXIX.** (1947)

Don Thomson, **Men and Meridians: History of Surveying and Mapping in Canada.** (Ottawa: Queen's Printer, 1966)

John van Nostrand, Roads and Planning: The settlement of Ontario's Pickering Township, 1789-1975 **City Magazine,** 1975

W.F. Weaver, **Crown Surveys in Ontario.** (Ontario Department of Lands and Forests, 1962, revised 1968)

About the Author

William Humber is the author of eight other books including definitive histories of baseball ("Diamonds of the North", Oxford University Press, 1955) and bicycling ("Freewheeling", Boston Mills Press, 1986) in Canada. He has co-authored a history of Central Public School in Bowmanville (1989) and written children's books on soccer and baseball. Humber is a Chair in the Faculty of Technology at Seneca College in Toronto and manages the college's national outreach in the area of energy training. His family has lived in Bowmanville since 1974 where wife Cathie, and children Bradley, Darryl, and Karen participate in all manner of activities.

Index

Abernethy's, ... 91
Adelaide (Australia), ... 66
Agger, Robert, ... 98, 99, 100
Ajax, ... 110
Akron (Ohio), ... 67, 80
Alexander, J.B., ... 66, 67
Allen, William P., . . . 52, 91, 122
Allin, Don, ... 123
Allin, Miss Florence, ... 66
Allin, Harry, ... 91
Allin, Rev. W.N., ... 66
Alma Hotel, ... 43, 48
America, ... 1, 2, 29
America (steamer), ... 44
American Civil War, ... 46
American Revolution, ... 9
Antarctica, ... 2
Apple Blossom, ... 111, 113
Apple Festival
  and Craft Sale, ... 119
Arctic, ... 2
Armour, Robert, ... 46
Armstrong, Hattie
  Seymour, ... 60, 122
Aspen Springs, ... 115
Astor Photo Studio, ... 91
Atkinson, Joseph, ... 104
Atlanta Braves, ... 48
Australia, ... 42

Bagnell, Lieutenant W.W
  (Bill)., ... 75, 79
Bailey, John, ... 44
Ballyduff, ... 55
Balmoral Hotel
  (Castle), ... 90. 123
Bank of Montreal, ... 19, 21,
  92, 123
Barber, Augustus, ... 17
Barber, George, ... 45
Barker, Reverend
  Cephas, ... 32, 33, 36
Barings Bank, ... 21
Barnum and Bailey's Circus, . . 72
Base Line Road, ... 117, 118
Baseball Hall of Fame, ... x
Battle of Bowmanville, ... 118
Battle of Waterloo, ... 42
Bay of Quinte, ... 6
Beech Avenue, ... x, xi, 30, 41,
  42, 44, 66, 75, 76, 93, 123
Beith, Alex, ... 49, 122
Belden *Atlas (Historical
  Atlas of Northumberland
  and Durham Counties),* 14
Bell Telephone Company, . . . 33

Belleville, ... 47
Belleville Clown Band, ... 79
Bethany, ... 103
Bible Christian Church, ... 32
Big 20 Bookstore, ... 91
Bismarck, ... 79
Blair, Charles, ... 52
Blake, Edward, ... 37
Bobcaygeon, ... 30
Bombard, Clarence, ... 81
Bonneycastle, Dr., ... 81
Borland, James, ... 27
Boston Bruins, ... 83
Boston Red Stockings, ... 48
Bowman, Charles, ... 11, 19, 76
Bowman's Village, ... 14
Bowmanville Bluettes, ... 79
Bowmanville Business
  Centre, ... 118, 119, 124
Bowmanville Cemetery, ... 39
Bowmanville Creek, ... xi, 2, 4,
  11, 116, 117
Bowmanville Fair, ... 30
Bowmanville Fire Hall, . . . 8, 121
Bowmanville Foundry, ... 81
Bowmanville Harbour, . . 84, 123
Bowmanville High 37, 73,
  School,   75, 81, 82, 99,
  122, 123
Bowmanville Legion
  Pipe Band, ... 79
Bowmanville Memorial
  Hospital, ... 87
*Bowmanville Messenger,
  The,* 25, 26
Bowmanville Ministerial
  Association, ... 84
Bowmanville Museum, . . . 21, 75
Bowmanville Owls, ... 75
Bowmanville Post
  Office, ... 92, 106, 123
Bowmanville Royal
  Oaks, ... 36, 48, 49,
  50, 51, 117
Bowmanville Royals, ... 81
Bowmanville Rubber
  Company, ... 67
Bowmanville Sons of
  Temperance Nine, ... 46
Bowmanville 8, 10, 93,
  Town Hall, ... 106, 121
Bowmanville
  Training School, ... 79, 81
Bowmanville Victorias, . . . 46, 47
Bowmanville Zoo, ... 109
Bradley Livery Stables, ... 55

Brampton, ... 64
Breslin, Dr., ... 89
British Columbia, ... 7
British Empire, ... 8, 32, 42
British 59th Regiment
  Foot, ... 42
British Isles, ... 76
British North America, ... 13
British Privy Council, ... 55
Brodie's Hotel, ... 56
Broken Front, ... 71
Brookhill, ... 113
Brown,—, ... 68
Brown, Bill, ... 123
Brown, George, ... 28
Brown Stockings
  Baseball Club, ... 51
Burden family, ... 47
Burden, Lyall, ... 69, 122
Burden, Samuel, ... 44, 47, 48
Burk (Burke), family, ... 13
Burk, John, ... 14, 76
Burlington, ... 15
Burt, Miss Grace, ... 59

C.M. Cawker & Son
  (butchers), ... 90
Canada, ... 43, 46, 48,
  58, 76, 83, 86, 91
Canada West, ... 8
Canadian Pacific
  Railway (CPR), . . . 91, 94, 117
Caer Howell House, ... 48
Campbell (family), ... 15
Campbell, ... 15
Campbell (daughter), ... 15
*Canadian Cricketer's
  Guide, The,* 46
*Canadian Statesman,
  The,* . . . . ix, xi,
  23, 25, 26, 27, 29, 31, 32,
  35, 36, 37, 38, 46, 47, 48, 50,
  57, 58, 60, 61, 78, 79, 81, 82,
  84, 85, 86, 87, 89, 90, 91, 92,
  93, 95, 96, 100, 106, 108, 109,
  . . . . 110, 117, 122
Candler, Bea (Mrs. Stuart), . . 76
Candler, Edward, ... 72
Candler, Elizabeth
  (Elizabeth Westlake)
  (Elizabeth Mitchell), ... 76
Candler, John, ... 71, 76
Candler, Samuel, ... 71, 72
Candler, Stuart, ... xi, 71, 73,
  75, 76, 86, 122, 123
Candler, William, ... 72

Captain Bill
(Six Nations), ... 46
Cann, Harry, ... 61, 62, 121
Carleton, Governor, ... 5, 6
Carleton Island, ... 6
Carlisle Avenue, . . 5, 44, 69, 116
Carruthers
(Mayor) Wilfred, ... 78
Casbourn, Harold, ... 123
Cass Baseball Club, ... 51
Caverley, Ken, ... 73
Cawker's Butcher
Shop, ... 42, 51, 122
Cawker, Mrs., ... 66
Central, ... 113
Central Public School, . . 38, 62,
72, 73, 74, 82,
94, 96, 115, 117, 122
Centre Street, ... 44
Ceylon, ... 76
Chapel Street, ... 14
Chase, Hon. Warren, ... 32
Chicago, ... 21
Childs, Joe, ... 69, 122
Christmas Tree Lighting, . . . 119
Church, Gardiner, ... 107
Churchill, Mary
(Mrs. W.R. Cubitt), ... 26
Cincinnati (Ohio), ... 51
Clan Macnab, ... 43
Clarington,
Municipality of, . . 17, 93, 106,
108, 110, 111,
112, 113, 114, 124
Clarington Corners, ... 115
Clarke, Sir James, ... 57
Clarke Township, ... xii, 2,
103, 105, 107, 118
Cleveland (Ohio), ... 79
Climie, George, ... 50
Climie, John, ... 26
Climie, William Roaf, ... 23,
25, 26, 27, 29, 32, 33, 34, 35,
36, 37, 38, 39, 44, 46, 47, 48,
50, 51, 58, 60, 117, 121, 122
Clinton Street, ... 14
Cluff, Nora, ... 60, 121
Cobourg, ... 11, 29, 42,
46, 47, 64, 93,
107, 108
Cobourg Cricket Club, ... 44
Cochrane, Ray, ... 79
Cole, Alma Piper, ... 60, 121
Cole, Gary, ... 91
Cole, Jack, ... 91
Cole, William, ... 75
Cole's Circus, ... 57
Coleman, Edwin, ... 50
Coleman, John, ... 5
Coleman Street, ... 14

Colville, Alec, ... 82
Colville, Bill, ... 82
Colville, Jack "Sandy", . . 82. 123
Colville, Katherine, ... 82
Colville, Mrs., ... 82
Collis and Reed, ... 111
Conants (Conats), family, . . . 13
Concession Street, ... 16, 43,
117, 118
Congregationalist Church, . . . 26
Congregationalists, ... 27
Cook, Mansfield, ... 60, 121
Cooperstown (N.Y.), ... x
Copeland, Lieutenant
Russell, ... 73
Cornstock, Johnnie, ... 5
Cotter, John, ... 27
Couch, Johnston &
Cryderman's Store, ... 90
Courtice, ... 107, 111
Cowan Block, ... 91
Cowle, —, ... 35
Crawford, Captain, ... 6
Cream of Barley
Mill, ... 17, 66, 79, 85, 123
Cross National Community Study
of Civic Involvement:
Some Empirical Findings
and Notes Towards
a Theory, ... 98
Cuba, ... 76, 80, 81
Cubitt, Fleetwood, ... 26
Cubitt, Colonel
Frederick (Mayor), . 23, 24, 26,
27, 29, 33, 34, 35, 36, 37, 38,
39, 43, 44, 45, 46, 55,
60, 117, 121
Cubitt, John, Churchill, ... 26
Cubitt, Richard (Dr.), ... 26
Cubitt, Woolmer
Richard (Dr.), ... 26
Czech Republic, ... 101

Danforth, Asa, ... 11, 15
Danforth Road, ... 16
Darlington Cricket
Club, ... 28, 44, 45, 49
Darlington Green, ... 113
Darlington Mills, ... xi, 14, 19
Darlington Nuclear
Generating Station, ... 71
Darlington Township, . . . xi, xii,
2, 3, 9, 14, 17, 26,
44, 46, 60, 64, 69, 71,
103, 105, 106, 107, 111
Darwin, Charles, ... 32
David Morrison
Senior's Orchestra, ... 83
Davidson,
Robert D., ... 52, 73, 122

Densem, Louis, ... 123
Descriptive and Statistical
Account of Canada, ... 14
Detroit (Michigan), ... 51, 72
Deyman, James, ... 52, 122
Dexter, —, ... 45
Diamond, Jack, ... 93
Diefenbaker, (Prime
Minister) John, ... 69, 83
Dickens, Catherine, ... 1
Dickens, Charles, ... 1
Dippell (Principal)
Louis, ... 82, 123
District of Newcastle, ... 9, 11
Division Street, ... 56, 90, 122
Dominion Bank, ... 30
Dominion of Canada, . . . 35, 37,
38, 42, 59, 68
Dominion Organ and
Piano Company, . . . 30, 38, 50,
65, 66, 67, 69, 91, 118, 122
Don River, ... 7
Donoghue, Bessie
Kilgannon, ... 60, 121
Dorchester, Lord, ... 8
Downey, Ellen, ... 59
Downey, Fred, ... 49, 122
Drill Shed, ... 5, 44, 47, 49, 69
Dudley, Ray, ... 37
Duke of Wellington, ... 42
Dunedin (New Zealand), ... 66
Dundurn, ... 42
Durham Board of
Education, ... 108
Durham County, ... xi, 9, 11,
46, 87, 92, 107
Durham Rubber Company, . . . 67
Durham Region
Offical Plan, ... 107
Dutch Christian
Reform School, ... 116
Dygert, —, ... 47

East Main Central Area, . . . 113
Eastern Ontario, ... 4, 48, 93
Eckfords Baseball Club, ... 48
Edinburgh University
(U.K.), ... 26
Edmonstone, G. Alex, ... 90
Edmondson, Mildred
Luxton, ... 60, 121
Egypt, ... 76
Elephant Hill, ... 113
Elford, Maude Wilcox, . . 60, 121
Elgin Street, ... 115
Ellesmere Road, ... 111
Elliott, Henry, ... 43
Elliott, S. Blain, ... 123
"Elms, The", ... 68
Emslie, Bob, ... 50

England, ... 14, 42, 59, 71
Enniskillen, ... 2, 30, 79
Erpingham (Norfolk, U.K.), . . 26
Etobicoke Creek, ... 6, 7
Europe, ... 83, 109

45th Battalion, ... 34
Fairbairn, James, B., ... 5, 14, 26, 37, 60
Fairbairn, Robert, ... 14
Fairbairn, Thomas, ... 52
Family Compact, ... 26, 29
Fenian (Raids), ... 44
Fenwick, ... 113
Ferguson, Alan, ... 123
Fice (Councillor) Wesley, ... 78
First Nations, ... 113
First World War, ... 66, 71
Fisher, Alexander, ... 21
Fisher, Carl, ... 123
Fisher, David, ... 21, 47
Fishleigh, Richard, ... 52
Fly Away (N.Y.), ... 48
Foster, Doris, ... 31
Foster, Fred, ... 31, 121
Foster, Mabel, ... 31
Four Corners of Bowmanville, ... 8, 10, 121
Fox, Alsay, ... xi
Fox, Thomas, ... xi
Four Freedoms League, ... 83
France, ... 5
Franklin Cricket Club, ... 46
Front Street Team, ... 61, 62
Furz, "Buzzy", ... 66

Galbraith Court, ... 117
Garret, Pete, ... 52, 122
Gaud, W.H., ... 55
Gay, John, ... 27
General Motors of Canada, ... 31, 100
Georgian Bay, ... 30
Gifford's Tannery, ... 15
Gill, Major, ... 81
Glen Rae Dairy, ... xi
Glover, —, ... 38
Goheen's Handy Store, ... 91
Golden Report, ... 107
Goldsmith, Fred, ... 50
Goodman, Clare, ... 52
Goodyear Glee Club, ... 66
Goodyear Ladies' Hockey Team, ... 61, 62
Goodyear Orchestra, ... 66
Goodyear Tire and Rubber Company, ... 67, 68, 69, 84, 94, 101, 122, 123
"Gossiper", ... 57

Grace, W.G., ... 51
Grand Trunk Railway, ... 27, 57, 59, 121
Grand Trunk Railway Station, ... 28
Great Britain, ... 13, 21
Great Farini, ... 45
Great Pine Ridge, ... 107
Great Reform Convention, ... 29
Greenaway, Leo G., ... 90
Guelph, ... 50
Guelph Maple Leafs, . . . 47, 48
"Gun Shot Treaty", ... 6, 7
Gunter, Edmund, ... 9

Hackenberger, Michael, ... 109
Haines, George, . . 24, 34, 35, 121
Haldimand Township, ... 107
Hall, —, ... 45
Hallman, Irene, ... 81
Hallman, Ruby, ... 81
Hamburg (Germany), ... 109
Hamilton, ... 21, 42, 47, 50, 76
Hamilton Standards Baseball Club, ... 51
Hamlyn, Rupert, ... 14
Hampton, ... 2, 43, 55, 56, 72
Hamre (Mayor) Diane, ... 111
Harriston, ... 51
Harvey, Irenie, ... 79
Hazelwood, Dr., ... 81
Head, Lady, ... 45
Head, Sir Francis Bond, ... 45
Helliwell, J., ... 45
Heward, J.O., ... 45
Higginbotham, Mr. Fred T., ... 80, 117
Higginbotham, Mr. T.E., ... 80
Highway 2, ... xi, 8, 14, 15, 93, 95, 105, 108, 109, 110, 116, 121
Highway 57, ... 107
Highway 401, ... 93, 117
Hill, Ken, ... 52
Hillier, Doctor Solomon Cartwright, ... 38, 42, 66, 79
Hillier, Mrs. Solomon Cartwright, ... 79
Hind, Ada, ... 56, 122
Hindes, Alphonso, ... 41
Hindes, —, ... 15
Hoffman, Dan, ... 67
Holland, ... 98
Holland, Major Samuel, ... 9
Holmes, John H., ... 45
Holt Road, ... 71, 112
Home District, ... 8
Hooper, Ken, ... 94

Hornung, Joe, ... 50
Horsey Block, ... 92
Horsey, Mr., ... 121
Horice (Bohemia), ... 98, 101
Hubbard, Pinkie, ... 52
Hughes, General John, ... 73
Hughes, Sir Sam, ... 73
Hull's Marsh, ... 44
Humber family, ... xi
Hunt Street, ... 117
Hunt, Willian (Bill), ... 44
Hunt, William Holman, ... 42
Hutcheson, St. John, ... 28, 43, 45
Hutchison, Bill, ... 123
Huxley, Thomas, ... 32

India, ... 90
Indian Department, ... 6
International Association (American), ... 50
International Harvester Company, ... 51
Iroquois, ... 4
Israel, ... 76

Jacob Nead's Foundry, ... 15
Jackman, Harry, ... 123
James, George, ... 79, 86, 87
James, Jesse, ... 72
James, John, ... 87
James, Moses A., ... 25, 36, 121, 122
Jeffery, "Jiggy", ... 66
Jennings, Minnie, ... 4, 73
Jewell, Mary, ... 94
Johannesburg (South Africa), ... 66
Johnson, Leo, ... 7, 19
Johnson, Samuel, ... 36
Johnston, J.H., ... 73
Johnston, Sir John, ... 6
Jones, Casey, ... 72
Jones, Ernie, ... 69, 122
Jury, J.H., ... 91, 121

Kaitlin Development, ... 115
Kawarthas, ... 83
Keith, Charles, ... 52, 122
Kent, Bob, ... 75, 105, 106, 123
Kent, Carl B., ... 52, 122
Kent, John, ... 42
Kerr, James, ... 55
Kidd, Fred, ... 52, 122
King, Ben, ... 69, 122
King, Dr., ... 57
King Leary, ... 81
King, Mackenzie, ... 32
King, William C., ... 41, 52, 92, 122, 123

King Street,......... 8, 20, 27,
        33, 51, 56, 65,
        86, 90, 92, 93, 95,
        104, 121, 122, 123
Kingston,............. 15, 16,
        47, 48, 50, 81, 82
Kingston Road, ... 4, 11,
        16, 23, 41, 55
Kingston Pen
        (Penitentiary),........... 21
Knight, H.J.,.............. 66
Knox,.................. 113
Krug, Peter, ... 118
Kunstler, James, ... x
Kydd, Mr. Frank, ... 80
Lake Iroquois,.............. 2
Lake Ontario, ... 2, 4, 6, 9, 12,
        16, 46, 76, 112, 115, 121
Lake Scugog, ... 2
Lakeshore League,... 60, 81, 122
Lamb's Road, ... 109
Lambourne, Mark, ... 123
Lankester, Edwin,.......... 32
Laughlin, Mr.,............. 73
Laurier, Sir Wilfred, ... 69
Leetooze, Sher,............ 64
Leisure Lady
        Women's Shop,........ 51
Lewis, Lewis, ... 14
Liberty Street, ... 4, 16, 30, 37,
        80, 108, 112, 117, 122
Lindsay, ... 21, 30, 47
Lions Centre,......... 30, 95
Lions Club, ... 75
Little, Scot, ... 64
Live Oak Baseball
        Club,............ 44, 47
Liverpool (U.K.),.......... 66
Livingstone, Ed., ... 50
Lloyd Ellis Shoe Store,...... 90
Lockhart, W.T., ... 37
London,.................. 50
London Atlantics, ... 50
London Tecumsehs, ... 49
Longboat, Tom, ... 79
Longworth, Harold, ... 123
Loscombe, C. Robert,...... 59
Loscombe, Mrs. R.R.,...... 68
Loscombe, Robert
        Russell,............. 24, 34,
        38, 59, 60,
        68, 121
Lovers Lane, ... 118
Lowe Street, ... 42, 44,
        65, 75
Lower Canada,............. 8
Lunney, Elsie,............. 14

Macdonald,
        Sir John A.,........ 28, 36, 38

Mackenzie,
        William Lyon, ... 26, 27
Macnab, Reverend
        Alexander, ... 43
Macnab, Allan Napier,...... 43
Madison, —, ... 45
Maher Shoe Store, ... 52, 91
Main Street, ... 52, 90, 123
Manning, Fred J.,...... 52, 122
Maple Festival
        and Antique Show, ... 119
Maple Grove,............. 82
"March Manyweathers",..... 57
Markborough Properties, ... 110
Market Square,..... xiii, 8, 121
Markham,................ 50
Mason & Dale Hardware,.... 91
Mason Cup, ... 62
Mason, George, ... 52, 62, 122
Massey, Daniel,........... 104
Mayer, Florence,........ 58, 122
Mayer, Markus,........ 58, 122
McArthur, Francis, F— .. 24, 29,
        30, 33, 34, 121
McConochie, R., ... 47
McCowan, Miss Amy, ... 73
McCoy, Garnet, ... 91
McCready, H., ... 121
McCulloch, —, ... 44
McDonald, Jim, ... 121
McFeeter's James, ... 24, 38
McGregor, D.A., ... 95
McGregor's Drugs, ... 91
McIlveen, Gilbert, ... 123
McKay's Mill,............. 17
McKinley Tariff,.......... 83
McLaughlin,
        Colonel Sam, ... 91
McLaughlin Factory,...... 69
McLaughlin, Dr. James, ... 5, 30
McLaughlin,
        Mary (Mrs. Robert), ... 30
McLaughlin Touring Car,.... 31
McLaughlin, Arthur E.,.. 52, 122
McLaughlin, Robert, ... 30
McLung, —,............. 38
McTavish, Malcolm,....... 46
McMaster University,....... 98
McMurtry (family), ... 46
McMurtry, W.J.,.......... 47
McQuinn's, ... 91
Mearns Avenue,.......... 109
Meath, Clarence, ... 49, 122
Medd, Miss Alice, ... 81
Medland home, ... 4
Medland, Miss,.......... 121
Memorial,............... 113
Memorial Clock Tower, ... 82
Memorial Park
        (Bowmanville),.......... xii

Merchant, The,............ 57
Methodist Episcopal
        Church,............... 44
Middle Road, ... 109, 116
Milne Distillery,.......... 15
Mississauga, ... 65
Mississauga(s) (Indian), ... 6, 7
Mitchell, John B.,... 52, 65, 122
Mitchell, Lindsay,......... 123
Mitchell, R.M.,........... 66
Moffat, Rolly,............ 21
Mohun, Frank,........... 84
Montreal, ... 1, 14, 19, 21, 43
Montreal City and
        District Savings Bank,..... 19
Moorecraft, John,...... 52, 122
Morden, James
        Lake,........... 66, 85, 123
Morey, Cloyd,............ 52
Morris, Lieutenant, ... 80
Morris, Miss Helen, ... 72, 74
Morrison, David, ... 14
Morrison, David Sr.,........ 15
Morrison's Goodyear
        Orchestra,............. 66
Morsehead, "Mousy", ... 66
Moses, Horace "Bub",...... 123
Moscow (Russia),.......... 66
Mosport Race Track, ... 86
Mostert, Richard,......... 109
Mostert's Greenhouses,..... 109
Moynes (son),............ 43
Moynes, Issac, ... 43
Mr. Horsey's Grove,......... 4
Munson, Miss Charlotte, ... 55
Muskoka,................ 83
Mutton, Gladys, ... 60, 121

Napanee,................ 47
Nassau District, ... 8
National Geographic, ... 103, 112
Natural History
        Museum (Britain),........ 32
Neads, Elizabeth, ... 61
Neads, Nina,....... 61, 62, 122
Neads, Wilson,............ 61
Neville, Charles, ... 44
New Age,................ 32
New England,............. 93
Newcastle,... 46, 48, 83, 93, 99,
        103, 104, 105, 106, 110, 112
Newcastle Beavers,...... 46, 48
Newcastle Citizens
        League,............... 83
Newtonville, ... 55
New York
        City, ... 21, 58, 116, 122
New York Clipper, The,...... 50
New York Fly Aways, ... 48
New Zealand,............. 42

North America, ... xi, 5,
    44, 47, 78, 108
North American
    Indian Shamanism, ... 32
Northbrook
    Development Group, ... 108
Northglen, ... 113
Northumberland
    County, ... xi, 9, 11,
    46, 92, 107, 108

Oak, "Wally", ... 66
Oak Ridges Moraine, ... 115
Observer, The, ... 5, 32
Oke, Wilbert, ... 81
Old Scugog Road, ... 2, 55,
    109, 116
Old Swamp Angel
    Baseball Team, ... 50
Omemee, ... 103
Onagara, ... 6
Ontario, ... ix, xi, 1,
    4, 7-9, 11, 13, 14,
    16, 21, 44, 45, 50, 71,
    101, 102, 103, 107
Ontario Association
    of Architects, ... 119
Ontario Bank, ... 19-21,
    30, 92, 118, 121, 123
Ontario Hockey
    Association, ... 21
Ontario Hydro, ... 80
Ontario Lord's Day Act, ... 84
Ontario Municipal
    Act (1849), ... 11
Ontario Rifle Association, . . . 80
Ontario School Act (1846), . . 11
Ontario Street, ... 59
Ontario Training School
    for Boy's Band, ... 79, 86, 123
Opera House, ... 101, 123
Orono, ... 23, 50, 55, 103
Orr, Bobby, ... 83
Osborne, —, ... 68
Osborne, Al, ... 75
Oshawa, ... 11, 19, 21, 30, 51,
    65, 69, 78, 81, 83, 90,
    92, 95, 101, 104, 105, 107
Oshawa Generals, ... 83
Oshawa Times, ... 110
Oswego (N.Y.), ... 83

Palm Readers and
    Counsellors, ... 90
Parkway Crescent
    Sub-division, ... 93
Pattinson, Nellie Lyle, ... 37
Payne, Fred, ... 123
Pelican Card Club, ... 51
Pepino, Jane, ... 108

Percy, John, ... 68
Percy, Miss Regina, ... 80
Perrin, Bill, ... 52, 122
Perth, ... 21
Peterborough, ... 108
Peterborough Majorettes, ... 79
Pethick Brothers, ... 68
Pethick, Edward, ... 42
Pethick, Frank, ... 33, 121
Phare, Lance, ... 91, 122
Pickering, ... 11, 110
Picton, ... 81
Piltdown Man, ... 32
Pine Ridge, ... 2
Point Peninsula Culture, ... 4
Pollution Probe, ... 107
Pontypool, ... 103
Port Darlington, ... 76, 83, 113
Port Darlington
    Harbour, ... 30, 118
Port Darlington
    Harbour Company, ... 45
Port Hope, . . . 11, 21, 47, 49, 93
Port Perry, ... 47
Prince Street, ... 79
Prisoner of War Camp, . . 79, 118
Private Capital, The, ... x
Prospect Street, ... 115
Prower, William, ... 38
Public House License, ... 83
Pypker, Ralph, ... 75

Quarrington, Paul, ... 81
Québec, ... 8, 19, 21
Queen Street, ... 37, 59, 94
Queen's University, ... 87
Queen Victoria's
    Diamond Jubilee, ... viii, 121

R.M. Mitchell & Co., ... 91
Raby, George, ... 69, 122
Rafferty, —, ... 47
Rathskamory House, ... 30
"Ravenscraig", ... 66
Raynes, Elizabeth, ... 76
Region of Durham, ... 10, 103,
    105, 107
Regional Government
    Organization Branch
    (Ontario), ... 107
Rehder (family), ... 66
Rehder, Christian, ... 81
Rehder, Tom, ... 81
Reid, W.H., ... 37
Rhem, Ann
    (Mrs. John Candler), . . . 71, 76
Rice, Harry, ... 122
Rice Lake, ... 5
Richards, Alf, ... 69, 122

Richards, Gordon, . . 60, 121, 122
Rickaby's, ... 91
Rickard, Brenton, ... 123
Rickard (Mayor) Garnet, ... 92
Robertson, Heather, ... 30
Rochester (N.Y.), ... 46
Rolph, Thomas, ... 14
Rosicrucianism, ... 32
Ross Can Company, ... 66
Ross Can Sextette, ... 61
Rotary Park, ... 82, 95, 117
Rowe, Don, ... 123
Royal Theatre, ... 90
Rundle, Dr. H.B., ... 79
Rundle, Sid, ... 123
Rykert, C.J., ... 45

S.W. Mason & Son
    Dry Goods, ... 62, 91
Salvation Army, ... 56, 122
Salvation Army Band, . . . 72, 79
Sears Department Stores, ... 55
Second Street, ... 115
Second World War
    (WWII), ... 37, 76, 82
Selmon, Keith 123
Serling, Rod, ... 105
Scarborough, ... 93, 107, 111
Schickendanz
    Brothers, ... 109
Schofield, Jim, ... 51
Scobell, Edith, V., . . . 61, 62, 91
Scotland, ... 42
Scott, Lewis, ... 81
Scott, Miss, ... 72
Scott's Orchestra, ... 81
Scugog Street, ... 65, 80
Shaw, Miss, ... 66
Shaw, Thomas, ... 43, 46,
    47, 48, 50
Shaw, Wallace, ... 49, 122
Shaw, William Wesley, . . 58, 122
Short, Mrs. W.B., ... 66
Shrubb, Alfred
    (Alfie), ... 79, 83, 85, 123
Silver Street, ... 80
Simcoe County, ... 27
Simcoe, Lieutenant-
    Governor
    John Graves, ... 9, 13
Simpson, D. Burke, ... 21, 38
Simpson, John, . . . 14, 19, 21, 76
Simpson, Dr. L.J., ... 82
Six Nations Reserve, ... 46
Sixty Years of
    Canadian Cricket, ... 44
Slemon, Keith, ... 123
Smith, —, ... 15
Smith, Charles, ... 69, 122
Smith, Major, ... 34

Smith, Miss, ... 55
Somerscales, George
(T.V. Shop), ... 91
Soper Creek, ... 17, 117
Soper, Leonard, ... 17
Sousa, John Phillip, ... 72
South Africa, ... 83
Southey, Mrs. E.C.C., ... 81
Southey, Jimmy, ... 81
Speciality Paper
Products Company, ... 67
Spencer, Major, ... 76
Squair Grocery Store, ... 15
Squair, John, ... 1, 13, 14,
                              16, 26, 46
Stanley Cup, ... 80
Stedman's, ... 90
St. Helen's
(Oregon), ... 98, 100, 101
St. John's Anglican
Church, ... 28, 33, 42, 45
St. Lawrence Baseball
Club, ... 48, 49
St. Paul's Cathedral (U.K.), . . 42
St. Paul's Church, ... 37
St. Stephen's Catholic
High School, ... 118
Strike, Al, ... 21
Strike, W. Ross, ... 21
Summersford, Ken, ... 123
Sun, The, ... 36
"Sunrise", ... 37
Supreme Court of Canada, . . . 55
Sutton, Thomas C, ... 28, 45
Sutton's Barber Shop, ... 91
Swedenburg, Emanuel, ... 32

Tait's Camp, ... 80
Tait, H.C., ... 123
Tamblyn, Alan, ... 123
Temperance Street, . . . 8, 20, 50,
                  65, 82, 86, 92,93, 95,
                  106, 117, 121, 123, 124
Templeton, John, ... 48
Third Battalion of Durham, . . 45
Tilley, Mr., ... 76
Tilley, Mrs., ... 76
Tilley, Ross, ... 37
Tolkien, J.R.R., ... 68
Thickson, Miss Heloise, ... 81
Third Battalion
of Durham, ... 45
Thompson, Andy, ... 82
Thompson, William, ... 24
Thompson Knitting
Team, ... 61, 62
Toniato, ... 6
Tom Dustan's Hardware, ... 91
Toronto, ... x, 6, 7, 11, 16, 21,
                  26, 29, 30, 45, 48, 50,

51, 55, 59, 64, 69, 76, 78,
80, 83, 85, 89, 93, 95,
100, 103, 104, 112, 116, 121
Toronto and Eastern
Railway, ... 80, 81
Toronto Baseball Club, ... 21
Toronto Cricket Club, ... 45
Toronto Dauntless Club, ... 47
Toronto Globe,
The, ... 28, 45, 82
Toronto Granite Club, ... 75
Toronto Normal School, . . . 55
Toronto Purchase
Tready (1787), ... 7, 9
Toronto Star, The, ... 82, 104
Toronto Telegram, The, ... 52
Township of Cartwright, ... 31
Trebilcock, Mr. —, ... 121
Trent River, ... 6, 9
Trinity College, ... 41
Trinity United Church, ... 87
Trull family, ... 5, 12
Trull, Mrs., ... 5
Trussler, Mr., ... 73
Trzic (Slovenia), ... 98, 101
Tuerk, Fred, ... 81
Twain, Mark, ... 29
Tyrone, ... 41, 43

Underhill, George, ... 123
Union Cricket Club, ... 46
United Empire
Loyalists (UEL)
(Loyalists), ... 6, 13, 99, 100
United States, ... 6, 13, 30,
                              46, 86, 91
University of Toronto, . . 3, 16, 95
Upper Canada, ... 8, 9, 13,
                              15, 44, 103
Upper Canada College, . . 44, 45
Upper Canada Furniture
Company, ... 30, 47
Upper Canada
Rebellion, ... 27, 28

VanAmburgh's
Menagerie, ... 57
van Nostrand, John, ... 119
Vanstone family, ... 43, 76
Vanstone, W.G., ... 44
Vanstone's Hill, ... 4
Vanstone Mill, ... xi, 2, 4,
                  14, 15, 23, 75, 121, 123
Vanstone's Pond, ... 6, 80,
                              86, 116, 121
Venice (Italy), ... 104
Venton, Don, ... 123
Veltri Complex, ... 56, 122
Veltri, Mario, ... 92
Victoria Bridge, ... 43

Victoria Building, ... 90
Victoria Hockey Club
(Winnipeg), ... 80, 117
Vincent Massey, ... 113
Visual Arts Centre, ... 17
von Mullenhein, Baron, ... 79
Warnica, Lieutenant
Day, ... 73
War of 1812, ... 16
Waterfront Trail, ... 118
Watertown (N.Y.), ... 49
Wattleworth, C., ... 66
Watson, William, ... 43
Watson's Hotel (Orono), ... 55
Waverly, ... 113
Waverley Road, ... 117
Wellington Street, . . . 65, 74, 80
Werry, Benjamin, ... 44, 46, 50
Wesleyan(s), ... 32
Wesleyville, ... 103
West Durham, ... 37
West Durham Review,
The, ... 66
West Main Central
Area, ... 113, 114
Western Bank, The, ... 30
Westlake, Arthur, ... 76
Westnutt, Harry, ... 122
Westvale, ... 113
Whitby, ... 11, 19, 21, 45, 47
Whiz Company, ... 66
Wickett, Greta, ... 72
Widdicombe, Dick, ... 72
Wilcox, Jim, ... 51
William, Alan, ... 122
Williams, Alan, ... 52
Williams Commission, ... 7
Williams, Gwendolyn, ... 81
Williams' home, ... 15
Wilson, Nell Piper, . . . 60, 121
Wind at My Back, ... x
Winnipeg, ... 80
Wood, Lou R., ... 51
"Wood's Senate", ... 51
Woodland Period, ... 4
Woodstock, ... 50
Woodward, El, ... 69, 122
World War Two
(WWII), ... 37, 102
Wright, Harry, ... 48
Wyoming (U.S.), ... 72

Yonge Street (Hwy 11), ... 9
York Region, ... 64
Young, Neil, ... 103
Young Ontarios
Baseball Club, ... 48
Yugoslavia, ... 98, 101

Zellers, ... 81, 110

9 781896 219219